CREATE YOUR PERFECT FUTURE

Heal your past to create the life of your dreams

Anne Jirsch *with* Anthea Courtenay

piatkus

PIATKUS

First published in Great Britain in 2013 by Piatkus
Reprinted 2014

A CIP catalogue record for this book
is available from the British Library.

ISBN 978-0-7499-5965-4

Typeset in Sabon by M Rules
Printed and bound in Great Britain by
Clays Ltd, St Ives plc

Papers used by Piatkus are from well-managed forests
and other responsible sources.

MIX
Paper from
responsible sources
FSC® C104740

Piatkus
An imprint of
Little, Brown Book Group
100 Victoria Embankment
London EC4Y 0DY

An Hachette UK Company
www.hachette.co.uk

www.piatkus.co.uk

For Oliver and Luca –
you are the future

CONTENTS

ACKNOWLEDGEMENTS

I would like to say a big thank you to all my FLP practitioners who have believed in me and helped me to develop my work and take it out into the big wide world.

A huge thank you to Dr Paul McKenna for your wisdom, encouragement and advice.

And my sincere thanks to: Paul Duddridge for your advice and knack for knowing the right thing to say; Dave Brown for once again being the most amazing subject to work with; Robert Kirby, the best agent ever; and Anthea Courtenay, for all your hard work and wonderful input.

Finally, my special thanks to Dr Rupert Sheldrake, for giving permission to quote from his work, and to Dr Dean Radin, the Barefoot Doctor and Laurelle Shanti Gaia, for their contributions, as well as to Paul Craig, Lilian Hulf, Jan Taylor, Paul Stevens, Pippa Jackson, Kreet Rosin, Sayaka Carndorf, Tomoya Nakamura and Marianne Bøeor for giving their time for interviews.

Anne Jirsch

FOREWORD
BY PAUL McKENNA

I keep meeting people who have been in therapy for years and can tell you everything about their problems, because they 'understand' them now. But none of the therapy has made the slightest difference to their behaviours or happiness.

I am certainly not saying there is no value in traditional therapy; it's just that it tends to take a long time and, overall, has very poor results. What Anne Jirsch provides in this book, however, is an opportunity for you to heal any core elements of your psyche that were formed in the past and may be holding you back or stopping you from having a more amazing future than you have ever dreamt possible. Her deceptively simple set of techniques work using the power of your imagination, which affects the unconscious mind – the unconscious mind being the larger mind, which keeps you breathing, your body regenerating and is the source of your creativity and wisdom. The unconscious also controls all of your thoughts and behaviours, and the best way to communicate with it is through the imagination. This is why hypnosis or visualisation exercises are so powerful.

Albert Einstein made many of his amazing scientific break-throughs while doing what he called 'thought experiments'. He would visualise atoms and molecules and gain profound insights into the nature of the universe. Indeed, he also said that if you want to know the future, then look at the past. Anne's approach not only embraces this concept, but uses visualisation to ask the genius bio-computer (your brain) to predict who, where and when you might be in the future. Whether you see the future or invent one as part of a 'thought experiment' is not so important; it is still undoubtedly a highly useful process.

Anne's approach to securing a happier and more fulfilling life is both psychological and metaphysical, but no belief in the techniques is necessary – just give them a go and notice how much better your life becomes!

Paul McKenna

INTRODUCTION

We are living in an age of massive change, some of it challenging, some of it truly exciting. And the rate of change is speeding up. People are becoming increasingly aware that there is more to life than the superficial: they know they can have, be and do more. They want the world to be a better place. The problem is they don't always know how to go about creating it. This book has been written to help them – and you – move forward.

In my career as a leading pioneer of Future Life Progression (FLP) I have helped many people to change their lives and find their true path. I am now about to demonstrate how to take an even bigger step forward. In this book I will explain how to use FLP not only to set about creating a better future for yourself, but also to clear any impediments from the past that may be preventing you from being so much more than you could ever imagine.

FLP is a process which helps you to choose your own future. No doubt you have heard of past-life regression, through which people are led into a light hypnotic state that allows the mind to travel back to childhood or a past life. FLP enables you to look into your future, also by using a light hypnotic or meditative state, together with other techniques that let the mind travel forward in time. These techniques work with incredible accuracy to show you not only your future, but a choice of possible futures depending on what action you take. I have written about them extensively in my book *The Future is Yours* and will be describing some of them here.

After I started working with FLP I discovered many further techniques, mainly guided by my intuition and inner wisdom. But somehow I knew there was more for me to learn; I did not have the whole picture. For several years I meditated and asked for an answer. Finally, the breakthrough came by way of a very special visitor from the far distant future, who gave me the knowledge contained in this book. This was a major turning point for me, as it will be for you, when you learn how you too can gain guidance from the future.

At that time, many of my clients were telling me they felt stuck or held back. They had worked hard on themselves, but some problems kept returning. Many of them had seen great results with FLP and had already improved their lives but, like me, knew they had so much more within them. They wanted to be the absolute best they could be; they wanted to contribute more and help to make the world a better place for themselves and others.

My visitor from the future showed me how people are held back by the past, often struggling vainly to clear longstanding issues. She taught me how to find the source of any lingering problems and then release them, and how, once free of the past, we can go on to create a far better future – in fact, a perfect future.

I have used the new information and techniques with both

individual clients and seminar groups, and the results have gone way beyond my earlier experiences. Clients all over the world have reported dramatic, positive changes in their lives, especially with problems that seemed to recur over and over again; finally, they were clear to move forward. If you follow the guidelines in each chapter, you too will be free to move forward to a far better future.

MY EARLY SPIRITUAL PATH

My spiritual journey began when I was a small child. I would sit at my grandmother's knee as she read the tea leaves for her eager customers in the East End of London. It all seemed so colourful and exciting. At that young age I heard all sorts of things a child shouldn't hear, but that just made me even keener to develop a skill of my own. I decided by the time I was eight years old that I wanted to be a psychic, just like my nan. The problem was I didn't appear to have any natural ability. Try as I might to have a premonition, nothing ever happened.

In my teens I vowed to find out how intuition worked, and to develop my own. Getting information was difficult in those days. We didn't have the internet or the vast array of spiritual books we see in bookshops today. I soon realised that to find what I needed, I would have to travel. So in my late teens I set off for the mystical centre of the world – India. At that time India was in the media because the Beatles and other famous people were heading there to meet gurus and to gain enlightenment. It was the place to go if you wanted to develop your spirituality.

Truthfully, I was pretty naïve. I expected to sit at the feet of some amazing guru listening to pearls of wisdom and assumed 'it' would all happen in the blink of an eye. In fact, I found myself sitting on a mat beside a very wise old beggar on a dusty roadside in Calcutta. Vikram taught me so much about intuition and how time works. He taught me about creating energy, and through him I became fascinated by reincarnation and past-life regression. His teachings made total sense to me and helped me to open up my psychic abilities.

On my return, I resolved to uncover my past lives. This was, in fact, much harder than I had expected; regressionists were few and far between, and it was a number of years before I had my first session.

By then I had met my next spiritual mentor, an incredible woman called Greta Gill. To this day I have never met anyone like her. Tiny, yet full of energy, she seemed to have a direct line to the Universe. Everyone who met her was touched by her warmth and insight. The spiritual path was still pretty new to me, but through Greta I met a whole range of fascinating people who would talk at length about their experiences and give me advice.

One of them, an astrologer named Shelley, had been regressed to several of her past lives. I could hardly breathe as she recounted her visions of having been a slave girl in one past life and a rich merchant in another. Now I was even more determined than ever to be able to access other lives. I pleaded with the Universe to find me a good past-life regressionist and my request was answered when I discovered a flyer advertising a past-life workshop in London with the famous American regressionist Denise Linn.

Together with my best friend Terri, I attended the event on

a swelteringly hot day. Throughout the day I experienced several past lives, but the one that made the biggest impression was my first, in which I saw myself as a young black lad in North Africa. It was very odd to see myself with the long arms and legs of a gangly African teenager. The vision was short: I watched myself as I walked inside my home – a small hut – then, suddenly, a knife penetrated my abdomen. Next, I could feel myself floating out of my body and looking down on myself. It was not upsetting – much like watching a movie – and it left a big impression on me; now I knew I simply had to give this experience to others.

By now I was also becoming a competent Tarot reader (to this day, I still love working with the cards which 'speak' to me), as well as studying meditation and hypnotherapy, while remaining unwavering in my desire to work with past-life regression. For several years I looked for training, but just as I'd struggled to find a good regressionist, training was proving even more elusive. Luckily, however, I had built up a willing bank of clients to practise on and I discovered I instinctively knew what to do. Soon my clients were undergoing wonderful and profound past-life experiences.

That was my life for over twenty years – working with Tarot cards and past life regression, while fine-tuning my psychic abilities – until one day, two young soldiers dropped into my little office in Slough for a regression session. From that day on my life changed for ever.

THE SOLDIERS

Steve and Dave had a deep fascination with regression and they proved to be such outstanding subjects that I began to work with them regularly, always curious as to what the next session would reveal. Over weeks and months they uncovered many past lives they had shared together, sometimes fighting alongside each other, at other times against each other.

I took them through my past-life training and they both became excellent past-life regressionists.

One day, in 2001, Steve told me, 'Dave and I have both seen you in our practice sessions. We've all known each other before.' He added, 'I have a feeling there's a reason why we have met again this time around.'

I'd had the same feeling myself and decided to find some answers. I brought in one of my best past-life students to take all three of us back to the life we'd shared together, to see if it held any clues. My student Dan began skilfully guiding us back to a previous existence connecting all three of us – but instead of going back in time, something strange happened: we all simultaneously jumped forward to a future event. At the time it made no sense to us; then, two weeks later, on 11 September, our visions were to become a shocking reality.

As we watched the scenes of the Twin Towers collapsing on our television screens, exactly as we'd foreseen, we were horrified. If only we'd seen more; if only we'd known enough to stop this terrible event. The question was: could we do this at will? Could we see future events in detail? Suddenly everything between us fell into place, and we knew we had work to do.

From that moment we began experimenting to see if we could predict more world events. Our results were consistently accurate. Within a fortnight Dave had predicted, among other things, that America would invade Iraq looking for weapons of mass destruction.

DISCOVERING FUTURE LIFE PROGRESSION

It was time to begin experimenting again, using a similar process to past-life regression, but now taking clients a few years into the future. Again, the results were amazing. They would see where they would be living, the people who were in their lives and how their work was progressing. Soon they were calling me to report that what they had seen was happening – but the remarkable thing was that events they'd seen many years ahead were happening much sooner than expected: things they'd seen occurring in five or ten years' time would happen within months or even weeks. Clients were rapidly meeting their ideal partners, getting businesses off the ground and even resolving issues with their health or finances. In many cases, they had seen more than one possible future, enabling them to choose the best for themselves.

I realised that we were not just seeing the future; somehow we were fast-tracking our futures. It was as if the very act of seeing them was bringing them forward into the now; as if bringing an event into our current consciousness enabled it to happen. Christopher's story, below, is a perfect example.

Christopher's Story

Christopher was a hard-working man, but, as he put it, 'success always seemed elusive'. He had a steady but boring day job which he tried to escape by trying out various part-time businesses in his spare time. Though he had some small successes they were never enough to enable him to move full-time into something more productive and exciting. He felt he was treading water.

I took Christopher forward five years to see what he would be doing: he was still in the same dull job, though his part-time business as an acupressure therapist was growing – albeit slowly. We moved forward another five years: he'd now packed up his day job and was working full-time as a therapist. He'd added a few new skills and gained a lot of experience.

I asked him how he felt, expecting him to be pleased with how things had turned out.

He replied, 'Well, I am ticking over, but I still worry about paying the bills each month. I am struggling along and would have expected more by now.'

I then asked him what he could have done differently. He told me, 'I needed to be braver, to push myself forward more. I can now see that I've always had a lack of self-belief and that has held me back. But at least I am no longer in that job.'

So I asked Christopher to feel, fully, what it was like to be working full-time at his chosen career, to keep that feeling with him and bring it back to his present time.

A few weeks after the session Christopher called to tell me, 'Some extraordinary things have happened! I thought a lot about what had come up and somehow "feeling" how things would be in the future made me feel like that right now. Does that make sense? As soon as I began to "feel" it, it began to happen. I've had a flood of clients, and I know this will grow. I expect to pack up my day job within six months.'

Three months later Christopher had indeed packed up his day job and was now working confidently as a full-time therapist.

Once you can connect in this way with the future events you desire, you bring them into your current consciousness by creating the energy needed for them to happen.

An example of this was in my early days of working with FLP when I took a close friend five years into the future. He told me about his future career success and wonderful home. He then added: 'I see you with a three-book deal.' At that time, the publishing industry was cutting back, and only the very famous would get a three-book deal. Within weeks, however, as well as my friend being offered the amazing business deal that he'd seen and finding his beautiful home, I'd 'by chance' met my agent and had soon secured a three-book deal.

Now all this was supposed to take place five years into the future, yet everything we had seen had happened in less than one month! I cannot promise that things will always happen that quickly – in fact, this was exceptional – but over and over again I have seen clients fast-tracking their future success and even love.

TOWARDS A BETTER FUTURE

So much happened as a result of that day in 2001 when I first discovered FLP through a vision of the events of 11 September with my soldier friends. I began to receive daily messages from grateful clients reporting how their future visions were happening in record time. FLP had given them the knowledge to take the correct path – whether in their work, home or love life – and head in the right direction. The sessions had stopped them wasting time and had energetically brought their future forward, and they were very happy.

When my book on the subject – *The Future is Yours* – was published in 2007, it became an international bestseller. I received enquiries from all over the world from people who, having bought the book, read about me in the media or seen me on television, now wanted to experience FLP for themselves. I could not be everywhere, though, and so decided to offer FLP training to a few trustworthy people who were already experienced professional therapists in other fields. I now run the world's first FLP Training School with over 250 therapists in eight countries, and we are growing fast, from Estonia to Japan, from the Middle East to America and Australia.

Meanwhile, I was also being consulted by business leaders, Hollywood A-listers began to call and I was even whisked off to a palace. Before long, FLP was showing the way for some of the world's most influential people.

Even so, something was niggling: deep down I knew there was even more to discover. Yes, people were fast-tracking into the future, but my instincts told me there was far more to it than they realised themselves. In many cases I could feel something holding them back from reaching their full potential.

My clients come from a very wide range of backgrounds, but there was something many of them seemed to have in common. Overall, they were happy with their lives – a number of them were even successful in some areas – but these clients still had at least one stubborn problem that wouldn't shift, no matter how hard they tried. For some it was money-related, while for others there was a love or health issue. Many had recurring problems that they'd tried to clear with various therapies and treatments, but no matter what they did the issue remained stubbornly unchanged. Some even had multiple blocks that refused to budge. They'd worked relentlessly on themselves, but the same issues were repeating themselves over and over again.

The question was: how could I take my clients beyond whatever was limiting them? I knew they wanted to be, to have and to give more, but something was allowing them to progress only so far. I resolved to find the answer: how could I clear their way to an even better future – to the life they were meant to be living?

From working with FLP I knew the best place to find answers was in the future. For my third book, *Cosmic Energy*, I spent a year taking trips into the future to discover what we will know in a hundred, even two hundred years' time that we need to know right now. I discovered a wealth of information. I could see our future selves unburdened by blocks and at peace with themselves, and I was determined to discover their secrets.

During my first session working with this aim in mind, I became aware of a very special presence beside me: that energy or being that sent great love and compassion to us all, that being from the future (see Chapter 2) that guided me and gave me the information that I needed. (I will be telling you more about this being in Chapter 2, and throughout the book.) I was shown an image of a road that broke into several pathways towards the future. Then I was shown how our past can pull us back. I saw people struggling to move forward, but being pulled back to where they'd started from, as if by a giant elastic band.

Next, I was told that not only our future but our past holds a number of different options. At first I had trouble getting my head around this concept, but then my companion told me, 'Ah, but you see, our past is just what we think we remember. It can be changed just as easily as the present and future; you just need to know where to look.'

In this book I shall be showing you just how to do that. But before we begin, please read the section below to prepare yourself for going through the exercises in the rest of the book, which will help you to achieve your aims.

GETTING THE MOST FROM THIS BOOK

There may be a burning issue in your life, such as a lack of love or money. Once you have read the first two chapters, feel free to go straight to the chapter you most want to work with. Each of the remaining chapters includes a number of exercises, but do be aware that often there is an overlap whereby one issue can affect another, even if it's not at first obvious. For instance, someone who has persistent money problems may need to clear an issue to do with love, such as feelings of unworthiness. So by working through the whole book you will enhance all areas of your life.

When you read my clients' stories you will see that in some cases I say that I take them back to the past or forward in time, which I do using either past-life regression or FLP respectively, under light hypnosis. You will be able to take yourself back to your own past and forward to your potential future by using the exercises I shall be giving you throughout the book, such as the Three Passageways (see pp. 14–17) and the Buggy (see pp. 55–57).

PAST OR FUTURE

Some of the exercises in the book work on the future and others are for clearing the past. So before you get started, think about what you would like to gain from this book. Write down your thoughts and feelings. What do you want? What do you need? What would you like to change?

Now look over your notes. If you have written something along the lines of: 'I want to stop attracting difficult moody partners', or, 'I would like to get out of debt or get away from this area', these are statements about moving away, and to do this you will need to do work on clearing the past. If you have written about wanting to get a better job, start a business or meet a positive partner, you will need to do the forward-looking exercises.

In either case, I would recommend doing the Three Passageways exercise (see pp. 14–17) first, to make sure. I often work with clients who tell me they have no problems relating to the past, only for us to find a huge block that we can easily clear. Then we are ready to move forward to create a better future.

HOW TO BENEFIT FROM THE EXERCISES

During the exercises, you will be asked to do some visualisation. Although in actual fact, we all visualise all the time, occasionally, I meet people who believe they can't. In such cases, I will usually ask them, 'What colour is your front door?' And when they respond, without hesitation, I go on: 'You had to visualise your front door in order to know the answer. Even if I ask you your telephone number, you will visualise it so that you can tell me.'

Your dominant sense

While it is true that everyone builds images in their minds, for some people their other senses are more dominant. A way to discover your dominant sense is to stop for a moment and think about your last holiday or trip. Take a few minutes to write a paragraph or two about it.

Once you have finished, look over what you have written and notice how you have described it. If your dominant sense is visual, you will have used more visual expressions such as 'It was beautiful', 'We looked out over the sea', 'We watched the sunset'. If you are more of a 'feeling' person you will describe how it made you feel – 'It was so relaxing' or 'peaceful' or 'hectic'.

Now some people are more 'thinkers' and they tend to give you a lot of facts, such as, 'We arrived late at night', 'Our hotel room was on the twelfth floor', 'It was expensive', 'It was a large resort', or perhaps they will recount the history of the region. If your writing is more fact-based, then you are more of a thinker.

As you work with each exercise your dominant sense will tailor how you experience it. So if you are more visual you are more liable to see images in your mind's eye. If you are more 'feeling' you are more liable to say, 'I feel I am outside', or 'I get the feeling I am with someone'. And if you are a 'thinker' you are liable to experience thoughts or ideas popping into your mind without effort.

The key is to allow the information to flow; do not censor it or think 'I am just making this up'. The mind has a way of trying to make logical sense of things; just put the doubting side of your mind to one side and allow the information to come to you.

If a client says they are worried that they are making up what they are experiencing, I usually ask them, 'Have you ever thought about this before?' Invariably they tell me, 'No. It has never occurred to me.' Just know that your own subconscious mind can access all the information that you need – trust it, and allow it to do its job.

Pointers

- Before starting an exercise, make yourself as comfortable as possible. You may sit or lie down, whichever you prefer.

- Dim the lights and perhaps have some soft new-age music playing in the background.

- Make sure you will not be disturbed; turn off your phone and do the exercise when you have plenty of time to spare and are not under pressure.

- Use your own judgement on how long to spend on each exercise, but if you are unsure, do less rather than more. You can always come back to it another time.

- You may do the exercises as often as you wish; but occasionally, if you have been working on some deep-seated issues, you may wish to have a break of a week or two to allow yourself to process what you have experienced.

- You may wish to use one of the downloads on my website (see Resources), you could ask a friend to read the exercises to you or you can record them for yourself. If you do choose to work with one of the downloads and need more time at any point, you can pause the recording and still stay relaxed, then resume when you are ready.

- If you are dealing with a difficult or deep-seated problem, you might want to consult a qualified FLP practitioner (see Resources).

Opening up and closing down

When you are practising any spiritual exercise it is important to open yourself up at the beginning of each session and close down at the end.

The opening-up technique below is the perfect preparation for all the exercises I will be describing in the book. It will relax you in mind and body, protect you and connect you to your higher self. It should be done before any of the exercises in each chapter and will take you just a few moments.

By opening up you are signalling to your subconscious mind and to the Universe that you are ready to begin. It will also protect you from any outside negative energies and distractions. After a while, you will find that you can do this naturally and easily, and each time you do it you will tune in more quickly and deeply.

Closing down after every exercise will ground you and bring you back to Earth. You will be able to process the information that you have just gained, while feeling strong and focused.

By consciously closing down you are signalling to your subconscious mind and to the Universe that you have completed your exercise and are now ready to carry on with your day. This will ground you and complete your session.

Sometimes people feel a little light-headed after meditating, and by closing down properly you will feel back in the real world.

OPENING UP

You can do this sitting or lying down – though if you choose to lie down, make sure you don't fall asleep.

Find yourself a comfy place to settle – a bed or chair – and really sink in. Now take a few long, deep breaths. Each time you breathe in, think the word 'love' and with each breath out, think the word 'release'.

As you breathe in you will be breathing in a loving positive energy. As you breathe out, know that you are releasing any negative thoughts, feelings and emotions, allowing yourself to gain knowledge that you need for your own benefit.

Now imagine a white light shining down on you, protecting and surrounding you with love. The white light will stay with you throughout your exercise.

Know that the white light is connected to the Universal energy that knows all ('Universal energy' being what some readers may think of as God, the Source or whatever higher power they believe in). Every single piece of information is stored here and you will now have access to that information. Allow it to flow to you, bringing you what you need to know.

CLOSING DOWN

After each exercise allow your breathing to become regular and feel most of the white light slowly drawing back towards the Universe. It has done its job – it has looked after you.

Sit quietly for a few moments and breathe deeply. As you breathe in, feel your body and mind being energised and cleansed. Then, as you breathe out, release any residual feelings or sensations that you no longer want or need. With each breath out feel yourself release any energy that is no longer required.

Breathe in and out at least five times. Breathe in cleansing energy and breathe out anything you wish to let go of.

Now imagine you are sitting under a shower: this particular shower is very special. Imagine a silvery white shower of energy coming from the Universe and washing over you, just like water cleansing you. You may even feel a little tingle as it works its magic.

As the shower ends, notice that a little of the white light still remains shimmering around you. It will protect you and keep you safe, and if at any time you need more universal love and protection it will draw more to you. But for now, this is all you need: a slight shimmer of light.

Finally, imagine yourself reconnecting with your everyday life, feeling your feet on the ground and your body strong. Now feel ready to move forward with confidence with your new knowledge and energy to guide you.

> Please remember to open up before and close down after every exercise.

KEEPING A JOURNAL

This book takes you into the past to discover what holds you back and it will take you into the future to explore your best possible future life. As you work your way through the exercises, it is a good idea to keep a journal to track your progress and to remind you of any ideas that come up for you along the way. You may find you use some exercises more often than others; and you may well find that you slip backward and forward in the process of clearing the past and creating your future before achieving the life you truly deserve. The journal will give you a log for future reference and help you to see what works best for you.

In your journal entries, make a note of:

- the date

- the technique you used and what you were hoping to achieve

- the result

- a reminder if you want to go back and use the technique again at a later date to see if anything has changed.

FUTURE LIFE PROGRESSION –
A LITTLE TASTER

To get a taste of FLP, you can try the following visualisation in which you take a look at London (or any place you wish) in ten years' time. It will put you in the right frame of mind for looking at your own future and using the exercises in this book. (This exercise is also available as a free download on my website – see Resources, p. 240.)

EXERCISE: LONDON IN TEN YEARS

Start by opening yourself up, following the instructions on p. xxix.

Now, find yourself a comfy place to relax and take a nice, deep breath. Take a moment to concentrate on your breathing and feel your whole body let go.

Imagine you are standing in the middle of a corn field. It is a beautiful day and you can feel the sun shining down on you, giving you a warm glow. There is a cool, gentle breeze; you watch the corn swaying from side to side and you can feel it brush against your legs. You can hear the sound of insects chirping around you and birds flying overhead. Enjoy the peace of your surroundings.

Suddenly, up ahead, you notice a small, round silver craft, sitting in the middle of the field. You walk through the long corn, and as you approach this craft you get the sense that it will take you into the future.

A door opens in the side of the craft: inside, it feels welcoming. You climb in and sink into a big, comfy chair, as the door gently closes.

You have a sense of moving upward as the craft takes you to a higher awareness to gain information about the future of London.

Next to you, you notice a control panel. You reach out and tap the screen and watch as it lights up. You see a section labelled 'Location', and you tap in the word 'London'. Now in the box underneath, labelled 'Time', you tap in '10 years'. The screen whirls and confirms you will now visit London in ten years' time.

You become aware of moving, and deep within you, you know you are moving forward in time. Feel yourself floating forward through the years: one year, two years, three years, four years, five years, six years, seven years, eight years, nine years and ten years.

You look down and find yourself floating over London, ten years from the present time. Take a moment to focus on this time and place. Be aware of what your senses tell you.

As you look down on the city, get a sense of how things are. What do you see? What do you know? What can you feel?

Get a sense of how London is doing financially. Is it thriving or perhaps struggling?

How are the people of London? Are they happy?

Look at the environment of London. Does it seem cleaner or more polluted?

Look at transportation – is travel easier? Cleaner? Are there any problems? Have there been any breakthroughs?

Look at the royal family. Have there been any new additions? Who is on the throne? What is the public feeling towards the royal family?

Get a sense if any one person or group is making a positive difference to London.

And finally, now that you have this vantage point, focus on this question: what do the people of London need to know right now in the present time?

Take a moment to see what comes to you.

And now take a deep breath and feel the craft beginning to move backward, until it reaches your present time.

Finish by closing yourself down (see pp. xxix–xxx).

Once you have tried this, I would love to hear your impressions. Do please post them on our Future Life Progression Facebook page.

Within these pages I will show you exactly how to clear the way to a better, shinier and happier future. I can see the human race rapidly evolving. We are ready for more. We are ready to grow, to have happier lives and to contribute more fully to the future of the planet.

My special visitor showed me the way and the wonderful news is that you also have someone from the future waiting to guide you and take you forward to a better and more fulfilling life. Soon I will be introducing you to that person.

Finally, we will look at how to create the best possible future for our world, a legacy for future generations.

You have more power over your own life than you can imagine, and with the right tools you can create the life you were truly meant to live.

CHAPTER 1

RE-WRITING HISTORY

Do you want a happier, richer and more fulfilled life? Since you're reading this book it's more than likely that you do. And you're not alone: wanting to improve your life is a natural part of being human. So why do some people find it so difficult? They may work on themselves by reading self-help books or meditating; some spend a fortune and sometimes years seeing therapists. They may dig up some childhood issues or perhaps clear some past-life trauma, and usually they will make some progress. Then, all too often, they suddenly find themselves back where they started, with the same old problems. Does that sound familiar to you?

HOW BLOCKS AFFECT US

One of my clients described his efforts as like trying to drive while stepping on the brake and the accelerator at the same time. Another said, 'I try everything, and I make some real progress. Then the same old situations repeat themselves and

I'm right back at the beginning.' It's rather like being a hamster on a wheel, frantically running and never moving forward.

Not everyone has this problem: I have often found that simply by using FLP to travel into the future it is possible to go beyond the time when a particular problem has been troubling you, and find that it has already been resolved. I've taken many people forward to a time when their issues no longer exist and their response has been: 'Oh! The upset feeling has gone. It's not there any more.'

A way to understand this is to think of something that used to worry or upset you years ago, and is now resolved. If you try to feel worried about it now, it will actually be quite hard. By going forward into the future we may bypass our current issues and automatically dissolve them. Once the emotional link is broken, the problem disappears.

However, all too often a pattern has become so deeply entrenched that past issues need to be cleared before we can move forward. Then we have to find the origins of the problem: where and when did it start?

Imagine someone with a phobia of spiders; throughout their life, they've panicked every time they've seen a spider. Now imagine a therapist trying to clear every single occasion when this has happened, one by one. Not only would it take for ever – it would also still leave the original cause untouched.

You could think of each time something like this has happened to you as a brick: over time the accumulation of bricks eventually builds a wall around you. You could try to remove each brick one at a time. But if you succeed in removing the first brick – the initial cause of the problem – the whole wall will tumble down. In other words, you do not need years of psychotherapy or self-work to heal your past: it is possible to free yourself now from blocks that were created long ago.

Changing the Past

Stephen Russell, better known as the Barefoot Doctor, is a world-famous teacher and practitioner of Taoism and the author of sixteen books on the subject. I asked him for his thoughts on how the past affects us, and whether it can be changed. He wrote the following:

> People routinely suggest we need to let go of the past. To me this is as daft as suggesting we need to let go of the ego. We need an ego, or structure through which to experience and operate in reality, in the same way we need to be connected to our past, otherwise we have no reference points and quickly lose our marbles.
>
> Just as the purpose of psychotherapy is to help the patient complete the ego, to retrieve all the split-off aspects, in order to function successfully in the world, we also need to honour the past and retrieve the connection to our primordial power as it was at conception, at birth, in the ebullience of infancy and so on. We have to honour the story that got us here. We have to own it – not let it go. For it's our past that's our wealth.
>
> What we have to let go of is belief in the sacrosanctity of the set of opinions, prejudices, beliefs and preferences acquired along the way, as these limit us in the present. And we can certainly elect to travel back in time, so to speak,

▶

and shift these opinions simply by altering the lighting schema and camera angle through which we're viewing the scene.

Whether this then actually changes circumstances and conditions in that time, which then affects the passage of time between then and the present and thus changes the present too, is an appealing metaphysical notion. At the very least, by revisiting past trauma and healing yourself from it, it balances you in the present too.

Paul McKenna gives an interesting exercise in his book *I Can Make You Rich*. He helps you to see a richer past whereby you imagine an alternative childhood, one in which you grew up with all the advantages of being surrounded by rich thinkers who believed in you, believed in your potential and had the financial means to put those beliefs into practice.

Paul says, 'It is simply a way of providing your unconscious mind with some new alternatives, so you will no longer be constrained by the limits of your old wealth programming.'

Everything you do and think is shaped by your own version of reality. You are the sum of your perceived experiences and your experiences are what you perceive as the past. Just suppose you could change that perception and thus your current reality. That is when things really begin to change.

A VISITOR FROM THE FUTURE

CAN WE CHANGE THE PAST?

Can we really change the past? Can we re-write our own history? I believe we can. It's not magic: we are continually creating our lives with our own consciousness. Just as a screenwriter writes a film script, our consciousness and our beliefs are creating our daily lives, and focusing on potential future events brings them about. But much more is possible: just as the screenwriter can go back and change a scene early on in the story, you can do the same. *You can re-write your life script to create a more positive past.* All you need to do is change your memories – and fortunately, memories can easily be changed, as I shall be showing you in the rest of this book.

THE NATURE OF TIME

Most of us have grown up with the belief that time is linear: that yesterday is behind us and tomorrow is still to come. We are taught from childhood to understand time as a straight line from past to present to future. Most people believe the past is fixed, many believe they have some control over their future and therefore it is variable, and some believe the future is set in stone.

Yet we have all experienced the feeling of time going very fast or slow or even standing still. Fred Alan Wolf is an American theoretical physicist specialising in quantum physics and the relationship between physics and consciousness. In his book, *The Yoga of Time Travel*, Wolf speaks of the 'timeless moment' that everyone experiences at some point: 'a period of quiet reflection when everything seems at peace. The reality of this moment surpasses the illusion of time.'

New theories about time started in the early twentieth century, when the celebrated scientist Albert Einstein proved that time goes at different speeds in different circumstances, and that past, present and future are not absolutes. This was the start of the study of quantum physics, which looks at the most microscopic particles which make up our world and universe. Since then quantum physicists have been coming up with all kinds of new ideas about the nature of the universe and time, many of which have been disputed by traditional scientists; indeed, in the early days quantum physicists had no way of proving any of their theories and often argued fiercely among themselves.

Theories about time introduced by quantum physicists include the possibility that the past, present and future are all happening simultaneously, or that time is circular with the past repeating itself; one thing they all seem to agree on is that no one really knows how time works. Among other quantum theories gaining in popularity is one that says everything is composed of consciousness rather than matter, and that there exist multiple parallel universes with slightly different realities happening at the same time – and that if we only knew how, we could jump into another, better universe.

'Quantum physics, very succinctly speaking, is the physics of possibilities,' says Amit Goswami, Ph.D., in the 2004 docudrama *What the Bleep Do We Know?* Goswami is one of today's revolutionary theoretical physicists who believe that science and spirituality can be integrated; he has developed a theory of survival after death and reincarnation.

One of the more recent questions under consideration is: can we influence the past? When I asked Dean Radin, author and researcher in the field of parapsychology and Senior Scientist at the Institute of Noetic Sciences, he replied, 'This is a common theme in time travel science fiction. The usual answer is perhaps. But if it is changed we'd never know it, because our present would be altered as a result of that change, and thus everything would seem perfectly normal.'

Time is not at all that it seems. It does not flow in only one direction, and the future exists simultaneously with the past.

Albert Einstein

Ponder the thought that if the past, present and future are all happening simultaneously, it is just as easy to influence the past as to influence the future.

ENERGY

Today you are the sum of your past experiences: every experience that has happened in your life has made you the person you are today and has given you the life you have now. At the same time, everything that happens to you creates its own energy.

All living things are surrounded by the energy body, known as the aura, which can be sensed and often seen by psychics and healers. It extends several feet all around the body in an oval shape, and contains a number of layers of shimmering, vibrating colours, which relate to different aspects of ourselves, from the physical to the spiritual. This energy body is affected by our own thoughts and feelings and by outside events and atmospheres; people who know how to 'read' auras can tell where there are problem areas and blocks in a person's emotional, mental or spiritual being.

You Are Energy

As you look up at the sky at night and observe the stars, just know that you are made of the same stuff; you are made of stardust. There is a part of you that is not your physical self; the part of you that is pure energy. This energy has been around since the beginning of time. Some people would call it the soul. Socrates himself believed the true self lies not within the body but in the soul.

You are made of pure energy that can transcend time and space, but know you have something extra, something special. You are energy with a consciousness that can reason and can bend time and that can create even more wonderful energy that will spread through your world and through the universe. You are pure energy but, oh, so much more!

A VISITOR FROM THE FUTURE

Negative experiences have a dense energy: just thinking about them leaves you feeling heavy and sluggish and depressed. Going through tough times can feel like walking through treacle: it's really hard to move forward, and time itself seems to go more slowly. And it is not only actual experiences that affect your energy: so do your thoughts and memories. Check it out for yourself with this simple exercise.

EXERCISE: CHANGE YOUR ENERGY

Focus right now on a difficult time in your life, maybe something that made you scared or anxious. Perhaps you were terrible at maths or sport at school, or as a teenager you were awkward with the opposite sex. As an adult you will still have a little of that energy residue with you. Find an incident from those times that you would like to change, and re-live it for a moment or two.

As you focus on that difficult time, pay attention to how you feel. You may become aware of a heavy, dense sensation. This dense energy of the past can weigh you down and hold you back for your entire life, recreating the same old patterns over and over again.

Now imagine that things were totally different and went incredibly well. Perhaps you came top in maths or excelled in sport. Imagine the admiration you received. Take a moment to really feel it. Bring yourself back to the present and be aware of how you feel in your current time. Notice the changes in your body. You will probably feel lighter and happier. In fact, just thinking about a more positive past brings about a total shift in energy.

Luckily for us, heavy energy can become lighter. By changing your thoughts and feelings you can change the density of any incident whether past, present or future, and by changing the energy of the past, you change the energy of your current time.

CHANGING YOUR PERCEPTIONS

One way to shift your present energy is to change your *perception* of the past, and this in turn helps to create a more positive future. People tend to believe that what they remember is the absolute truth. But very often, what we carry in our heads is merely our perception, our personal idea of what happened. Think back to a recent party or outing you attended with friends; as you discussed it with them afterwards each of you probably had a slightly different version of events, found it more or less enjoyable and remembered some incidents differently.

Here is a real-life example. Two years ago, on the eve of my friend Louise's wedding, she and her family were reminiscing about her life. Louise mentioned an incident in her childhood; she recalled an uncle saying she was an idiot as she practised for a dancing competition. With his words still ringing in her ears she did badly in the competition, and she gradually allowed her dream of being a dancer to fade. From that moment on, the mere mention of her uncle's name would unnerve her.

As Louise described the incident, an aunt with a good memory leaned over to her and said, 'But he wasn't talking about you at all! He was talking about his boss's wife who thought she was an expert on every subject under the sun.'

Louise told me, 'At that moment something lifted. To think that one chance remark has affected me for so long and to such a degree is shocking!'

She has now taken up dancing again, and although it's too late to make it a career she has certainly gained a great deal of pleasure from it. I have seen a real shift in her: she is more at ease with herself and has also recognised the importance of not being influenced by other peoples' opinions.

As soon as you decide to change a negative perception you can create a different past and begin to knock down the building blocks that have held you back.

IDENTIFYING PAST BLOCKS

Over the years I have found that blocks come from three sources: childhood, past lives or ancestry. The exercise on pp. 14–17 will help you to identify the initial block that applies to you and bring down the wall that prevents you from being all you can be.

CHILDHOOD

Childhood blocks can begin at birth and, sadly, many are picked up along the way. These are the kinds of block created by the parent who said you were stupid or useless, the teacher who told you that you would never get anywhere in life or the bully who made your school life a misery. They can come from witnessing your parents argue or go through a divorce, or from having a sibling who had health issues and needed all of your mother's attention. In fact, any difficult or stressful situation in childhood can result in blocks that will affect your entire life unless you identify and deal with them.

ANCESTRAL

Some blocks are ancestral; in other words they are inherited patterns and may have run through your family for generations. (There is evidence to show that these issues – or cellular memories – are locked into our DNA; research published in the *European Journal of Human Genetics* in 2002, as well as the work of Professor Wolf Reik at the Babraham Institute, Cambridge, confirms that the 'memory' of an event can be passed from one generation to the next.) For example, if your ancestral history includes a generation of Puritans, you are going to find it hard to cut loose and have a good time. And if in past centuries there has been great poverty, you will find it hard to create wealth.

We can identify these negative ancestral energies and clear them.

Inherited Memory

According to British biologist Rupert Sheldrake, 'Genetic memory is a process in which a memory is passed down through the generations without the individual having any firsthand experience about the topic of the memory.' Sheldrake proposes the idea that we inherit traits from our ancestors not only through our DNA, but by morphic resonance. He believes that all living things are surrounded by a 'morphic field' – a field of energy containing the memory of our inherited traits which are passed down to the next generation, then the next and so on. Groups of beings –

▶

humans, animals and so on – are linked by 'collective morphic fields'. He says, 'The idea is that there is a kind of memory in nature. Each kind of thing has a collective memory. So, take a squirrel living in New York now. That squirrel is being influenced by all past squirrels.'

This would help to explain why some people are born with special gifts, in music, the arts or mathematics, for example, which don't appear in their parents but may be traced to much earlier generations. Similarly, some of us suffer from fears or worries which are not relevant to our present lives but may have had genuine causes in the lives of our ancestors.

PAST LIFE

Imagine that you have been through lifetime after lifetime of difficult relationships. Maybe you've had heartbreak in many lives with one particular person. Or perhaps there has been a variety of scenarios when love has eluded you completely. It will be hard to have a loving and strong relationship unless these issues are cleared.

Or maybe you have spent many incarnations in poverty and hardship. How easy do you think it will be to create abundance if this is all your soul has experienced so far?

As you go through this book you will be learning techniques to clear past-life baggage and fast-track you to a happier, more positive future.

First, though, here is an exercise which will show you whether you need to clear past-life, ancestral or childhood memories. The Three Passageways is a key exercise in this book, as it enables you to discover exactly where problems arise in the first place.

Remember to open yourself up before you begin the exercise (see p. xxix).

EXERCISE: THE THREE PASSAGEWAYS

Find a comfortable place to relax, either sitting or lying down. Sink down and focus on your breathing, let go of your everyday life and allow your mind to be calm.

Imagine you are walking through a pine forest; the air is cool and clean and a slight breeze rustles through the branches. Up ahead is a clearing, and as you near it you can see in the distance a tall, snow-tipped mountain. As you look at it, you are aware that this mountain is very special; it has the power to show you your past.

You make your way to the foot of the mountain and notice a winding path leading to the peak which disappears among the clouds.

Step on to the path and make your way up the mountain. As you climb, you gain an increased sense of awareness; it is as if all your senses are heightened.

You come to a sturdy platform and you stop to admire the view. You look down over fields and a vast lake and you breathe in the cool, clean air. Time seems to stand still as you gaze over a snowy landscape and spot a beautiful little village surrounded by tall fir trees.

You recharge your energy to continue climbing up the mountain. Although the path is steep you are full of vitality, your legs are strong and you are enjoying the journey. You are now half-way up the mountain; you reach another platform and stop to enjoy the view. You can see more snow-capped mountains in the distance.

You feel at peace as you look around at the beauty of your surroundings.

You continue on your journey upwards and soon you are among the clouds; you feel them around you as you walk up one step at a time, until you are now above the clouds. You look out at the blue sky and up towards the universe.

The clouds begin to float away, leaving you with a breathtaking view. As you look out over the landscape you think about your life and how far you've come. You know you would like to make further progress and clear anything that blocks your path.

The pure, clean air refreshes your mind and brings you clarity.

You become aware of an elderly man by your side; he is wearing a white robe and has long white hair. He beckons you to follow him round the side of the mountain, and there you find yourself at the mouth of a cave.

You step inside and see that the cave is lit with flaming torches that cast a beautiful golden glow on the walls. As your eyes adjust you become aware of three passageways ahead of you. Each has a carved wooden sign above its entrance.

The sign above the first passage reads 'PAST-LIFE PASSAGE-WAY', the second reads 'CHILDHOOD PASSAGEWAY' and the third reads 'ANCESTRAL PASSAGEWAY'.

Stand in the centre of the cave and focus on the three passageways and on what you want to resolve. You may find that one stands out; it may pull you or repel you, or you may hear something as if it's calling you. It may even glow more brightly.

As you focus on the three passageways, be aware of any thoughts or feelings. Take time to be aware of what comes to you. How does it feel? You may be aware of feelings and emotions rising to the surface. Allow any sensations to flow. You may experience memories, good or bad; you may remember being a particular age, or a specific incident may stand out.

Now stand in front of the first entrance, the PAST-LIFE PASSAGEWAY.

Notice how you feel. What sensations are there? Do you feel calm? Happy? Do you see any images? Are you drawn towards this passageway? You may be aware of impressions of other times and places. You may glimpse an event from a previous life. Allow the information to flow to you.

Now stand in front of the second entrance, marked CHILD-HOOD PASSAGEWAY, and allow the impressions to flow to you. What are you aware of? Feelings? Images? Events? Are there any sensations? If so, what are they? What do your senses tell you? You may have a sudden flashback or memory. Do you sense that you need to enter this passage?

And now stand in front of the third entrance, the ANCESTRAL PASSAGEWAY, and again notice any feelings or sensations. You may suddenly think about your mother or father or grandparents. You may find yourself thinking of ancestors from way back in time, even those of whom you have no knowledge. Allow the information to flow to you.

Now step back and focus on all three passageways and notice which had the most dramatic effect, which drew you or repelled you the most strongly. Which did you sense you needed to visit?

That is the passageway you need to explore.

Your passageway

Focus on your chosen passageway and know that within it are the answers you need.

As you look down your passageway you notice a lighted torch at the entrance. The torch is showing you the way and guiding you to find the block that is affecting you in your current time.

Make your way down the passage: allow your instincts to guide you. You will reach a point at which you become aware of something – it may be a thought, a feeling, an image or perhaps something happening around you.

At this point stop and focus on the information that is flowing to you. Do not censor whatever comes; it is not necessarily what you expect. What you are aware of will be the origin of your block. You do not need to re-live it; you simply need to be aware of it.

*As you become aware, imagine you are peeling the block from you, as if you are taking off an invisible cloak. Cast it aside and say aloud, 'I do not need this in my present time.'

If you feel any resistance you can ask the resistance why it is there. You can speak to it. Usually it has been trying to protect you in some way. Tell any resistance that it can still protect you, but it now needs to stop blocking you from being all you can be.

Now say, 'I wish to take control of my own destiny.'

Walk back along the passageway and into the cave feeling lighter and fresher as you leave the block behind. Walk back down the mountain with a renewed sense of self and know that your life will be easier and abundance of all kinds will flow to you.

When you have finished the exercise, follow the instructions for closing yourself down, on pp. xxix–xxx.

[*We have several techniques for releasing the old energy. For straightforward issues the one described above will be fine. Later you will learn more complex techniques.]

Sylvia's Story

Sylvia had no idea why, as she put it, 'everything in my life turns to dust'; her love life, relationships at work, money – everything fell apart! She also told me she'd tried 'every therapy under the sun', and now believed she was just plain unlucky.

In order to uncover the original block I took Sylvia to the Three Passageways, where we found the information she needed.

As Sylvia stood in front of the passageways she hesitated slightly then said, 'I am very drawn to the ancestral passageway. I have no idea why – there is nothing relevant in my family's past.' I told her to go with it and see what happened.

As she walked along the passageway images flooded her mind, images of poverty and hardship. She suddenly felt a burning resentment of anyone with an easier life, something she'd never been conscious of before.

After the session, as we chatted, Sylvia told me that none of what she'd seen made any sense. I told her to just stay open-minded and to speak with some family members. She had experienced this for a reason.

Sylvia was still adamant that this was not a family pattern. However, later she questioned her mother and discovered that her grandparents had, in fact, had a similar pattern to her. They'd worked hard, saved money and taken care of their home, but every few years a catastrophe would occur to set them back. For example, their house caught fire; then her grandfather broke his leg in three places and couldn't work for over a year. The couple both developed a burning resentment towards anyone whose lives seemed straight-forward and easy.

Sylvia went on to discover more stories about her family history. She spent some time cutting the ancestral energy cords (see pp. 26–7), which enabled her to release the patterns from the past and to take a more positive path. The change in Sylvia was remarkable: instead of 'turning to dust', all areas of her life suddenly blossomed.

THE ETHERIC CORDS

There are a number of methods for clearing the past, but one of the most effective is cord-cutting (see p. 26–7). It quickly releases old patterning from childhood, ancestry or past lives. If you've read my earlier books you will be familiar with Etheric Energy Techniques. To recap: these days many people are aware of their auras and their vibration, but not everyone is aware of the more subtle part of their energy field: the etheric. This is a gossamer-like but powerful energy that surrounds your whole aura.

Some people miss it because they are so fascinated by the bright colours of the aura, but in many respects the etheric is more important: it is very powerful, and it can act as a protection. It can also stretch out to anywhere in the world and even the universe. In my workshops I teach techniques which enable your etheric energy to stretch out and reach a person you need to know about. Perhaps someone you love or care for doesn't seem too happy; perhaps you are wondering how they are feeling. As you tap into them you can gain useful insights. It is important that you only do this for the other person's benefit – for healing, for example – not in order to manipulate them or just out of curiosity.

Every time you interact with another person a cord is created between the two of you, and the more contact you have with someone the stronger and thicker the cord becomes. Energy flows along this cord – think of it as being like the umbilical cord between a mother and infant. It is through these cords that we connect with people and become attached to them. A problem arises when the energy flows just one way – for example, when love is not reciprocated. Another problem exists when the cords are attached between you and a negative person or situation.

There is nothing new about using your etheric energy to tap into others; most people do this without even realising it. Through the etheric cords we make connections all the time, not only with people, but also with places and situations which can last over many generations or lifetimes, often outstaying their welcome.

Cords are made of astral and etheric energy and connect two people's auras, stretching between them and transferring emotional energy and *chi* or life force. It does not matter how far away the other person is because the cord is not physical; you can transfer emotional energy just as effectively to someone you have a connection with on the other side of the planet.

Energy Vampires

The term 'energy vampire' is quite commonly used today. These are the people who, knowingly or unknowingly, use their etheric field to sap other people's energy. I'm sure you've had this happen; after speaking with someone for just a few minutes you feel utterly drained.

Cord-cutting can be useful to release that energy and break their etheric grip on you.

CORDS THAT STAY ATTACHED

While many cords are positive – those that attach us to good friends, for instance – negative ones can be responsible for holding you back. Most cords naturally fade away when they are no longer needed, but at times a cord can stay attached long after we feel we have moved on. The following scenarios describe how cords can stay attached for too long.

Past love

Have you ever wondered why you or someone close to you simply cannot let go of an old relationship even though it is long over? We all know someone who has been fixated on an ex, constantly obsessing about them, wanting to know their every move and every detail of their new life, even though it is sheer torture for them to hear.

Perhaps you've experienced this yourself; maybe you've been in a relationship which you knew deep down was wrong for you. But somehow you are still attached; there is something tying you together – an etheric cord. The cords that remain long after a relationship has ended leave you with an energy of 'unfinished business'.

Parents

Probably the strongest bond of all is that between a mother and child: the cords between them begin to form before birth, in the womb. Throughout the child's early life the connection with the mother increases more and more. Then one day the child prepares to leave, or at least begin to make his or her own way in the world – but not all parents are ready to let go.

By gently releasing some of the cords, both parent and child can move into the next phase of their lives. They will keep some of the cords and maintain a relationship that is warm and happy, but not as needy as when the child was younger and demanded more attention. (I will have more to say about this in Chapter 4, which is all about love.)

The 'nursie' syndrome

You may have come across people becoming irrationally attached to someone they hardly know or who have only played a small part in their lives. I've seen a good few men fall in love with their nurses when they've been in hospital; I've spoken to a few nursing staff who tell me they experience this on a regular basis. As the nurse has cared for the patient a cord has formed between them both. When it is time to go home the patient is still 'attached'; he has grown accustomed to the comfort and flow of caring attention from the nurse. Of course, this is a one-way street because the nurse has simply been doing their job and is now ready to release the attachment. Their job is done. The same thing can happen with doctors; usually the patient concerned will make up all kinds of excuses to visit the surgery in order to keep the attachment going.

I have helped a number of nurses and doctors release cords from patients who have simply not let go.

Celebrities

Today we see more and more people becoming 'attached' to people they don't even know, like TV soap actors or pop stars they have seen on television or in magazines – I am sure you've noticed the current obsession with celebrities. In some respects, this is natural, stemming from our primitive selves. As I zoom about on my travels into the future and past I see this phenomenon over and over again; it was necessary for our primitive selves, who were individually weak but became powerful in a group so long as it had a strong leader, and they would form a strong link to that leader.

Professional relationships

Most cords created casually are loose and weak and fall away quite naturally. But every time we make contact with a particular person we create a cord, and the more bonding the situation the stronger the cord. Every time you do business with someone you create a cord, and when people work closely together a great many cords can be formed and they become bonded. Similarly, therapists of all kinds can find themselves becoming very close to some of their clients in a short period of time; I know I have. A bond of trust is very powerful, and bonds can be misused by both practitioners and their clients. This is where cord-cutting can be beneficial. I've also seen business people become very attached to their staff, so that when an employee decides they need to move on to further their career, the boss can become distraught and act almost like a jilted lover.

People who affect your self-esteem

It's quite common to compare ourselves unfavourably with other people. It's often a close friend or a sibling; you are fond of them, but they seem wittier or cleverer or more attractive than you, so you feel belittled in their company. This often goes back to childhood, particularly when parents show a preference for one child, because they are brighter or better-looking or more talented than the other or others. Some siblings spend their lives trying to compete with each other or feeling resentful towards the favourite. Once you recognise the negative cords that have been created in this way, whether with a sibling or a friend, you can use cord-cutting to release the negativity, and then perhaps continue with a genuine friendship.

The Stalker

Jessica met a man through a dating website. She told me, 'In the first few minutes I realised he was odd. He began telling me how life would be once we were married! At this point, we knew next to nothing about each other. The evening couldn't be over quickly enough. Stupidly, I'd let him know where I worked and the next day a huge bouquet of flowers arrived,

▶

then the next day another. He started phoning me at my office every hour. I had just applied for promotion, but could see the bosses giving me odd looks. In desperation I did the cord-cutting exercise and – hey presto! – in an instant the phone calls, texts and flowers stopped.'

CUTTING THE CORDS

We have looked at a number of ways in which cords are formed; they are a normal part of our existence and, in the main, are a positive force of energy, as when someone sends you loving thoughts, healing energy or simply good vibes. The opposite is true of negative cords that drain you and hold you back. As I have said, we form cords all the time and the longer the relationship and the closer you are, the stronger the cords will be. As relationships end, the cords naturally fall away, which can sometimes take a while. But at times they can have a damaging effect on you. This is when cord-cutting comes in.

Often you will be able to easily identify where you need to cut a cord relating to your present life. However, if you have recurring issues, these are a sign that the problem originates in the past. This is when you need to investigate and use the Three Passageways exercise to find the source of the problem (see p. 14–17).

Past cords can come from our childhood, past lives or ancestry, and they manifest in our current time as physical, mental and emotional problems. Once you release them you will wonder how you ever survived with such a drain on you! You may have wondered why you repeatedly attract a negative type of person or situation into your life: etheric cords can keep you tied to a pattern lifetime after lifetime, and the longer you have had them the stronger they have become. You may have tried many methods to release the pattern, but while that cord is still attached the pattern remains.

Luckily, there is a simple method for releasing these energies.

Once you have identified the origin of the issue that needs to be cleared, through the Three Passageways exercise (see p. 14–17), you can use the following exercise to clear it.

You can either stand up for this exercise or relax and imagine you are standing.

EXERCISE: CUTTING THE CORDS

Before you start, open up, following the instructions on p. xxix.

Now stand (or imagine you are standing) tall with your legs apart at shoulder width and your arms hanging loosely by your sides. Make sure your back is straight and your feet are firmly on the ground.

Take a moment to be aware of the ground beneath your feet and the sky above your head. Be aware of your past and your future and remember that you are the sum total of all that has happened to you as a soul. Know that you are a timeless being.

Be aware of the issue that has been holding you back and that you are now ready to clear. Spend a few moments focusing on the issue and how it affects your life.

Now focus on your own energy and become aware of the cords

and energies that connect them; give yourself time to do this, and stay aware of how you feel. What areas of the body are you aware of? That will be where the cords are attached. You may feel the cords as a flow of energy, you may see them, you may just know they are there.

The cords may be thick or thin. They may have a heavy or light density. Notice where they are attached to your body – they can be attached anywhere. Any areas of your body that are carrying excess weight may have cords attached to them; it is as if the body is trying to build a barrier against the negative effect. Notice how positive cords energise you and negative cords drain you.

You may be aware of many cords, some of them positive, but the one you need to cut will stand out. It may be the only one you are aware of. Get ready to sever that cord.

The cord you want to release may have become very thick and strong, so you will need something very sharp and powerful to cut through it.

Imagine you are holding a big pair of silver scissors. These scissors have a laser-like energy that glows: it is very powerful, pure and cleansing. Hold the scissors, feel their weight; think of yourself as a surgeon making sure his instruments are clean and sharp.

Now take a nice deep breath in and, as you breathe out, cut that cord. Use your instincts to judge where to cut and then visualise the scissors cleanly and evenly cutting through the cord.

As you cut, breathe out fully, saying the words 'I release you.' Often my clients smile as they say these words and visualise cutting the cord.

Remember to close yourself down at the end of your cord-cutting exercise (see pp. xxix–xxx).

Selena's Story

I received an urgent message from Selena, asking for a Skype session. She sounded at the end of her tether. She told me, 'This might not sound like a big deal to others, but I love my horses and riding is my biggest passion in life. Yet I keep making excuses not to ride my horse. At times, I am on my way to the stables when something stops me, and I turn around and head home. There is always a logical reason for heading back, but I know I'm actually stopping myself.'

Selena told me that she'd had 'plenty of therapy', but nothing had resolved the issue. She was now at an age when, if she didn't clear it, her competing days would soon be over. 'Why do I stop myself from doing the one thing I love?' she asked.

We needed to find the root cause of this problem, so I took Selena to the Three Passageways. Her session was one of the most dramatic I've ever conducted. It was like a blockbuster film.

As she stood in front of the three passageways, Selena chose the ancestral route. As soon as she entered the passage, images flooded to her. She told me, 'I am aware of my grand-mother. I can feel her fear right now.

'My grandmother was Russian, and during the Second World War she had to leave Russia. She fled to Estonia and became a nurse. There she married an Englishman, my grand-father, and they moved to England where she was held in a camp for six months because they thought she was a collab-orator ... But I can feel I am going to go back further. I am being led further down the passageway.'

After a pause, Selena continued: 'I am aware of many

generations before my grandmother. I am aware of fighting. I can feel fear. I can see horses.'

Selena stopped speaking and so I prompted her, 'What is happening?'

Now she seemed to be speaking from the point of view of a man, a Russian villager. 'Our horses are strong. This makes us afraid. When our horses are strong we are attacked and they are taken. They come and beat us and sometimes kill. If our horses are weak they leave us alone. We must not let our horses become strong – it is safer that way.'

Selena went on to describe how a nearby nobleman would send his thugs over to attack the villagers and take what they had; he was especially interested in horses. If the villagers' horses were weak he tended to leave them alone and attack other, richer villages.

I asked, 'So how could things have been different for your ancestors?'

Selena thought for a while, then said, 'They could have concentrated on other ways to become strong, maybe with their crops or trading. They were so filled with fear about the horses that it consumed them, but they only needed a couple of horses. The nobleman was only interested in sleek, fast horses; the villagers could have built up the work-horses instead. Fear held them back.'

I told her, 'Talk to your ancestor and tell him what you have just told me.' Selena spent some quiet time communicating with her ancestor. She described seeing realisation dawn on his face: he knew that what she was saying made sense. He told her they would now 'lie low and be cleverer'.

Next, I got Selena to cut the cord connecting her to the fear. It was not her fear and had no place in her life.

Afterwards Selena said, 'I feel very different now, like something has lifted. This all makes so much sense to me. I've always had a fear that if I have anything, someone will come and take it from me. I feel now I can ride my horses and I know nothing bad will happen.' She laughed. 'Well, I am certainly not going to be attacked by warring noblemen, that's for sure!'

MEMORY

Many people are held back in life by negative memories in their present lives, often going back to childhood. In this book I want to show you how these can be recreated; we can re-write the past. In fact, people often do, without realising it.

Several years ago I spent the day with a mother and daughter who were known for their feisty arguments. Deep down they adored each other; nevertheless they constantly clashed.

I was with them once when they began to squabble about something that had happened a few weeks earlier, over the arrangements for the grandparents' wedding anniversary party. They argued over who had agreed to do what, and the daughter insisted that her mother had said terrible things about her own sister. It was odd to hear their totally different accounts of what they'd said to each other, and how they'd both reacted.

The mother was upset by the daughter's accusations: she was convinced that her duaghter was totally misquoting her.

The daughter gave a completely different account of what she'd said and told her mother how she remembered the conversation. The mother was aghast that her daughter's version was so different from her own. Now, I have no opinion either way as I wasn't with them when the words were originally spoken, and have no idea if either of their accounts was accurate. What was clear, though, was that they both believed their very different memories were totally correct.

This incident made a big impression on me about how memory works, and how unreliable it can be, even when we think we remember something perfectly.

Most of us tend to think of our memories as existing somewhere in our brains. We also tend to think they are stored in a particular place – as if our heads contain a kind of library or filing system, holding memories that are completely accurate. However, scientists have made some interesting discoveries that turn this kind of thinking upside down, particularly since it has become possible to view images of the brain in action while subjects are recalling memories of different types.

Daniel L. Schacter, Professor of Psychology at Harvard University and a leading researcher on the memory, has written and edited a number of books and published over 200 articles on the subject. In his Memory Lab at Harvard, he combines psychological techniques with scanning the brain, using PET (positron emission tomography) and MRI (magnetic resonance imaging) scans. He has found that far from being precise replications of the past, memories are 'reconstructions' of past events, which could better be thought of as collages or jigsaw puzzles than tape- or video-recordings. His work includes research into how the brain distorts memories; the book *Memory Distortion: How Minds, Brains, and Societies Reconstruct the Past*, edited by Professor Schacter, includes contributions from eminent scholars in a range of fields, from neuroscience to religion.

Despite research like this, nobody has yet discovered exactly how memory works. It is not found in one particular place in the brain – indeed, some researchers believe that memories are held in the cells of our bodies, as well as our minds. What we actually recall is influenced by all kinds of things, particularly our emotions; some people have real difficulty in letting go of distressing memories. Psychologists are working on methods of helping sufferers from post-traumatic stress disorder (PTSD), whose symptoms include flashbacks which replay frightening events as though they were happening in the present.

As Professor Schacter has found, some of the memories we believe to be true become distorted over time, for all kinds of reasons – they may have been painful, we may want to forget something we feel guilty about or we may want to recreate for ourselves a happier childhood or a more successful past than we actually had.

Elizabeth Loftus, Professor of Psychology and Social Behaviour at the University of California, also finds that we distort our memories, often by improving them. She says: 'Our memories have a superiority complex.' For example, an article in the *Guardian* in September 2008 described how Loftus has found that people remember getting better grades at school or giving more money to charity than they actually did.

How Accurate Are Our Memories?

You would think that for anyone present at a major event or disaster the scene would be etched indelibly on their memory, but the tragedy of the space shuttle *Challenger* in 1986 tells us otherwise. The morning after the disaster, psychologist Ulric Neisser handed out a short questionnaire to his students at Emory University in Atlanta. The questionnaire asked students to describe where they were, what they were doing and who they were with when the disaster occurred.

The completed questionnaires were kept for three years. Then Neisser tracked down forty-four of the participants to do another questionnaire just like the first. The aim was to test the accuracy of so-called 'flashbulb' memories of historic moments.

The results were shocking. Twenty-five per cent of the students now had very different memories of what had happened. Some of their memories differed in every detail; others had different versions of parts of the events. Yet the students were so sure their memories were accurate that they insisted their previous report, written just one day after the disaster, must have been wrong. There it was in their own handwriting, written while the events were clear in their minds, but now they were sure that the reports were wrong.

Taking this a step further, if you experience an event but are told enough stories about it that give it a different slant, will this alter your own memories? Will you end up having completely different images in your mind when you think back to the event – in effect 'recording over' your own version with the memories from other people's accounts? From Professor Loftus's research (described below) it seems that is what happens.

RE-WRITING MEMORIES

In the 1990s Professor Elizabeth Loftus carried out a major study in which participants were asked to read descriptions of events that happened to them as children. Unknown to them, one event was fabricated – a shopping trip when they were five, in which they got lost and were rescued by an elderly person. So susceptible were some participants to the simple but suggestive techniques used by the researchers that in their reports they talked about the event in detail, with self-assurance and emotion.

It seems clear that rather than being factual recordings of the past, memories are more like stories that we tell ourselves that can be made more vivid by the use of the imagination and encouragement from others.

Throughout this book you will find many exercises and techniques to help you to create a happier and more positive past once you have identified the block or blocks through the Three Passageways (see pp. 14–17) and used cord-cutting (pp. 26–7) to let go of it.

In the next chapter I shall be telling you not only how to let go of the past, but how to recreate it. By changing the past we can create a positive present to put you where you want to be now.

CHAPTER 2

A VISITOR FROM THE FUTURE

In the Introduction I told you how I discovered Future Life Progression and how it became my main area of work and focus. My second book, *The Future is Yours*, which tells the story and gives the FLP techniques in more depth, became an international bestseller.

At the time of publication I was experimenting with FLP and finding more great uses for it. On several occasions I looked further into the future – a thousand years to be precise. I wasn't expecting it to be like the movies with people wearing silver boiler suits, but I did expect to come across advanced technology, perhaps space travel, and hopefully the world in pretty good shape. But what I saw was beyond my comprehension. I was aware of outer space and galaxies and other realms, but my main awareness was of beings – highly advanced beings.

Up until then I had travelled a lifetime or two ahead and had been able to gain a good insight into how things will be, but this was harder to get to grips with. The things I would usually look at and the questions I would normally ask were not relevant in this future time. It seems that our selves in a thousand years' time are beings of pure energy. I could hardly ask them where they lived and worked and what they watched on television.

I discovered that I could communicate with them telepathically and, tentatively, I asked them where they were and what their purpose was. They told me they were pure energy but could take form, and that they used their energy to help people, planets and galaxies.

I asked them how they did this and they showed me bolts of light, by means of which they could create and send energy to where it was needed. At the times when they took form, they visited planets to show the inhabitants the way; often, they simply helped by influencing people telepathically.

These were still early days for me and I was still busy using FLP with my clients to find their right career paths or future partners. I felt a little out of my depth dealing with such advanced beings. I was unsure what to ask and when I did, although I understood some of their answers, I simply didn't understand them all.

At this time I was about to begin my third book. I had lots of ideas – but what would be the right subject? I wanted to give out the best information; I wanted it to be fresh and full of new ideas. I pondered, what did we most need to know about?

So during one jaunt to a thousand years ahead I asked the future beings for advice. They simply told me, 'Your new book needs to be about energy.' I pushed for more information and was told, 'You are not ready for our information just yet. Seek it out nearer in time.' They then vanished and did not reconnect with me for quite some time. But I did take their advice.

For a year I took regular trips a hundred, sometimes two

hundred years from our present time, on each occasion with just one question in mind: what do they know in the future that we need to know right now? During these time travels I saw how our future selves were using energy, and I discovered techniques that I tried out in my seminars and workshops. The results were incredible, and became the material for my third book, *Cosmic Energy*.

It was four years before I heard again from the distant-future beings, but this time there was a difference. I was ready to hear and see more. I was ready to be given knowledge.

THE VISITOR

I usually have my best ideas when I am walking beside the river near my home. During one of these rambles, I became aware of a presence by my side. Though I could tell that she was female, I couldn't see her clearly; I was just aware of a hazy glow. In fact, at first I could sense her rather than see her. She felt kind, giving out a great sense of peace, yet at the same time she felt powerful.

I wasn't sure who or what this presence was, but she stayed with me for an entire day. All I knew was that she felt familiar; it was almost like having an old friend by my side, a wise friend who could give me guidance. As my mind began to clear, I realised that she was communicating with me, through images, feelings and thought transference. It wasn't until she began to fade before my eyes that I understood she was actually my own highly evolved self, visiting me from the far distant future. This was to be the first of many visits, and she had a lot to tell me.

On this first occasion, she explained that we are all being guided by our Future Selves who are bringing help to our planet and our own evolution – help that is urgently needed. It comes in a number of ways: for example, through telepathy, dreams and inspiration. They send us energy to raise our vibrational levels (as we advance spiritually, our aura, or energy field, vibrates at higher and higher levels, enabling us to reach higher levels of consciousness) and even to influence the ideas expressed in movies and television shows.

My look of surprise prompted her to add with a smile, 'Your screenwriters think they are so clever, yet often their ideas and plots are planted in their minds by their Future Selves. When the time is right, we release the knowledge to inspire you.'

Apparently, many of today's films and television programmes contain important messages. 'Many', she said, 'show you another way to be. There are many realms and you now need to know how to access them.' Then she added, 'Often people believe they are seeing ghosts or angels when they are actually being visited by their own Future Selves.'

Films Inspired By Our Future Selves

Our Future Selves find many ways to inspire us: one is through inspiring the writers of films and television programmes. There have been many popular and high-profile films based on altered realities, time travel and the possibilities of changing the past and the future. *Back to the Future* (1985), for example, was very

▶

popular in its time, and the idea that we can not only travel to different times, but that we can also influence the future and even the past has since become widespread. Movies like *Minority Report* (2002) and others outlined below show us the possible repercussions and enable us to understand the concept that time is not linear.

In *Groundhog Day* (1993), an arrogant weatherman finds himself re-living the same day over and over again, each day trying something new until he learns some vital lessons about what is truly important in life. Later in this chapter I will show you the Buggy exercise (pp. 55–7) which will enable you to travel back and forth, trying out different possibilities, until you get the exact result that you want.

The Butterfly Effect (2004) tells how a young man travels back into his troubled past to try and change the present, and discovers that the tiniest change has repercussions. The message from this film is that we can change the past, but need to be aware of how it will affect ourselves and others.

In *The Time Traveler's Wife* (2009) a man suffers from a genetic disorder that, when he is under stress, causes him to spontaneously jump into different times. In one such time he falls in love and attempts to stay there to build a future with his now wife. While the hero of the story, Henry, has no control over his time travels and often cannot get back to where he wants to be, with the exercises in this book you have complete control over all your travels both there and back.

My Future Self visited me again a few days later and this time things became clearer. I was more than just aware of her being there now; I could actually see her more clearly, and her presence was stronger and more powerful. It was as if she was allowing me to gradually connect with her.

I could feel that as well as being gentle and feminine, she was also very wise and compassionate. As I looked at her I could see she was tall, not solid, but composed of a translucent energy glowing with subtle, soft colours. I could see that she was a version of myself, but somehow softer and calmer. She also had a strength about her, a no-nonsense attitude. I knew not to waste her time on trivia as I had in my earlier encounters.

I asked her, 'What do we need to know?'

She told me, 'People are awakening to new possibilities and a new perspective of life and their place in the universe. They are realising that they create their own reality. Since the dawning of time people have believed that everything happened because of some outside force; they believed in various gods or entities and that if their crops failed it meant their gods were angry and they needed to appease them. Now they know that they are part of the universal collective and each can play a part in creating a better life for all.

'Our past selves were too insular; they only focused on their immediate surroundings. They were only concerned with survival; they had to be, otherwise you and I would not be here. As life has progressed people have become aware that there is a bigger picture. In the past they worked hard just to eat and live. Now they focus on having a better and more fulfilling life. They have a new awareness that there is more to existence, and that we all have far more control over our own and our collective destinies than we previously thought.

'The key to having a better life is to find your common goal and put all differences to one side. Is there anyone on Earth who truly doesn't want the world to be healthy, abundant and full of love? Everyone wants the same thing: it is only the past that creates problems. People argue over their views and opinions, but truly they know so very little, most things they believe are not true. Wise people know this. They remain open.' She added, 'You all have far more in common than you now know.'

I prompted her, 'What is it from the past that holds us all back?'

'It can be many things: your family patterns and beliefs, things that have happened earlier in your life, or perhaps further back in your timelines in past lives or through ancestral energy. I will show you how to clear these so that you can move forward. You in turn must show others the same.'

Keen to learn more, I tried to push her further, but she simply said, 'That is all you need to know.' She smiled and said, 'Your leaders only need to teach this message and all will be well; conflicts will be resolved. Instead of trying to change others or beat each other down, worry not about what others think and believe.'

She told me that our planet and our evolution are at a turning point; if we are to move in the right direction we need guidance. I felt humbled as she told me that my next book, the one you now have in your hands, will help bring this information to people. You, the reader, are ready for this information because you are already much more aware.

In a subsequent visit my Future Self explained that the human race is evolving at an accelerated rate; because of this we can now make a difference, not only to ourselves and our world, but also to the entire universe. The first step must be to help our home, our Mother Earth, which we have hurt and harmed. It is as if we have been indulging in an extravagant party and now we have to clean up the mess. We have been reckless, only living for the moment, never thinking of the long-term consequences of our actions. Now we are paying the price. It is time for the human race to grow up and become more responsible, especially for the sake of future generations and the survival of our planet.

'You are all here to learn and to serve, to ease suffering. Think of the times you have felt truly happy and joyful – were they not connected to others? Concentrate on creating a better future instead of recreating the past.'

She stared at me for a full minute then said, 'You all need to know that you are the link from the past to the future.' And with that she was gone.

Over the weeks and months my Future Self shared many more teachings with me, which I will be sharing with you throughout this book.

MY PRACTITIONERS MEET THEIR FUTURE SELVES

After we had met a number of times, my Future Self told me it was time for other people in my present life who had developed their spiritual awareness to meet with their Future Selves, who were ready to guide them. 'Some of you are now ready to listen,' she said.

I had already trained a number of Future Life Practitioners

and took a group of them to meet their Future Selves. Their experiences were strikingly similar to my own and they, too, were given powerful messages, not just to help them on their own pathway but also for the world as a whole. (I will share these world messages in Chapter 7, when we look at the future of the planet.) Below are descriptions of some of their experiences in their own words.

Earlier I described how I first met the soldier Dave, and our experiences with Future Life Progression. Since then Dave has been an important part of the FLP journey and over the years, whenever he is in the country, we have experimented together and gained many more insights.

As I connected more and more with my Future Self I knew Dave was the first person I wanted to have this experience. Of course he had seen his future self in his next and several other lifetimes, but now I wanted to introduce him to his far distant, highly evolved Self. As expected, the session was both powerful and informative.

DAVE

As I took Dave to meet his Future Self he said, 'He is just coming into sight, yet I cannot clearly see him. This is odd because he is not solid, but I can see the energy. He is very tall and made of a mass of different colours, kind of in form and yet not in form. My Future Self is reaching out for me. The energy is incredible.'

'What is your impression of him?' I asked.

'He feels very peaceful but knowledgeable.'

I instructed Dave how to connect energetically with his Future Self and as they did so I could see a slight vibration flowing through him. He said, 'I can feel my entire body vibrating. It is the most amazing sensation. I can feel it, left to right, up and down; a vibrating energy. It is like a piston sending a mass of vibrations through me.'

I told him, 'You can adjust the flow.'

Dave said, 'Yes, I have done it, I have calmed the flow. I can control it as well as the flow of information and my thought processes.'

Dave sat quietly for a while and I could still see his body gently vibrating. I could also tell from the look on his face that the sensation was positive.

He told me, 'It's almost as if I cannot feel my body now. I feel just energy, pure energy. This takes me out of my everyday self and into another realm.'

'Does your Future Self have anything he needs to tell you?'

'Yes, he is telling me that the world is changing because we are changing. The people will make the changes come. They will make the world a better place. The real change comes from the people. He will tell me more on another occasion.'

'Ask him if you have a role here on Earth, and if so what is it?'

'To survive intact and to go out better than I came in. That is the whole point; anything else is a backward step.'

'What is your own personal next step?'

'To move forward and take action, action that has come from quantifying what aspect is more important than others. This is what gets in the way. We all need direction of purpose. You may have one thing that you class as more important than others, but certain aspects of your personality will hold you back and stop you from focusing on what is really important. The key is to not allow yourself to be held back. My purpose is to be informed and then inform.'

He then said, 'We will be talking often and he will guide me. I can't wait to see what happens next.'

I couldn't help but be struck by how Dave described his Future Self as 'in form yet not in form', and how his mission was to 'inform'. Somehow this was a key word. We will be hearing more from Dave later in the book.

PAUL

'Physically I was taller, seven to eight feet tall and I was dressed in white robes,' Paul said. 'I looked strong and broad and I had a taller forehead. My Future Self got down on one knee to talk to me. He put one hand on the earth, which seemed important. He had piercing blue eyes that had a real knowing behind them. I was aware that he had a huge energy.

'I was very respectful to him and kept wanting to call him "Sir" (I felt this was a male energy, but also universal). He didn't want this and found it amusing; he asked: "Would you call yourself Sir?"

'I felt like a child in his presence, like I was very immature and not developed in some way.

'His advice to me was: "Be yourself, be fully you. Do not worry about the meaning of all things, as this is not for you to resolve once here. Simply use your intuition as a compass needle to show the way. Know it is the journey towards knowing that is important.

'"Rip up the written plans, plan less and move in a real-time, inspired, more creative way. Intuition is THE direction to follow. Surf your thoughts and enjoy doing so, no second guessing and over-analysing. Just meditate more and get clarity on your actions for the day."

'I asked him what I needed to do. He told me, "Take more risks. That is how things move forward."

'He showed me as a sapling and told me I should be in the light, for I will then grow into the oak that is him. If I shun the limelight and keep my gifts and offerings in the dark it will take longer to become him. Lessons not learnt in this life will repeat themselves as challenges in the next and may even grow in size.

'I asked him, "Why am I here?"

'He replied, "To fail and succeed and fail and succeed. There are lessons that are equally for your growth and for others'. Look around: every year nature takes risks, nature grows where it shouldn't and gets cut down, but it also succeeds more and finds light and nutrients that make it thrive. You must do the same."'

LILIAN

'I was aware of a Light Being of silver, white and gold: a shimmering person, much taller than me. I was much as I am now, only more grown and evolved.

'I asked for guidance and was told that I am to follow what I do now, to keep healing and to keep letting go of crappy things and blocks, and of the blocks inside my body. Then I will balance and let go of fear and negative connections to past lives. I will then become an example of how to do this and can teach others to do the same.

'I was then told, "We are contacting the forerunners and you are one. Use your wise woman energy."'

JAN

'My Future Self looked much bigger than me, taller and broader with a bigger forehead. It was like I was pure shimmering energy of a much higher vibration, a blue-white iridescent colour, but at the same instance it seemed like we had all escaped our forms. I reached out to my Future Self and it felt like a physical jolt to touch.

'I am not sure if my Future Self was male or female, but I knew they were very wise and very compassionate and had learnt through past experiences to reach the ultimate level of knowledge.

'I was told that it was important to be me, and be true to me – to remember who I am and then forget who I am.

'I asked, "Why am I here?"

'I was told: "To help others find direction and help clear the blocks that get in their way and prevent them from being happy."

'My Future Self told me that I am already on the right track. I now need to follow what I've already seen and to look out because more signs will come.'

Many people are now ready to meet their Future Selves. In recent times a number of people have gained a great spiritual awareness, and some appear to have rapidly evolved. The fact that you are reading this book shows that you have the necessary awareness: on a spiritual level you are ready.

EXERCISE: MEETING YOUR FUTURE SELF

Find a comfortable place to relax and make sure you will not be interrupted; ideally, choose a time when you do not have to dash off anywhere, perhaps late in the evening or on a Sunday morning. Start by opening up, according to the instructions on p. xxix.

Spend a few moments concentrating on your breathing and if any thoughts come into your mind, just imagine them floating away. Clear your mind in readiness.

Now visualise yourself in a beautiful forest. It's a crisp autumn day; the sun is reflected in a gently flowing brook. You are enjoying a relaxing stroll through the forest, the crisp golden leaves crunching underfoot.

You watch a grey squirrel with a big, bushy tail dart swiftly up a tree and disappear into the branches.

It's a very peaceful time here in this forest and you enjoy gently walking along, breathing in the sweet, fresh air. As you meander through the trees you notice the beautiful colours of woodland flowers and soft green moss growing on the fallen tree trunks.

You see several leaves floating down from a tree and dancing in the air before fluttering slowly down to the ground.

As you stroll, you think about your life and how far you have come, and you ponder on where you are heading in life and all that you need to know to get where you want to. Sometimes life has been easy and at other times hard. At times you may have wished you had your very own guardian angel with you.

You pause for a while and rest against an old oak tree. You can feel the rough bark of the tree against your back and it is strangely comforting. You can smell the earthy ground and the freshness of the air. And as you rest here against the tree, you can feel a deep sense of peace in this beautiful place.

It is a beautiful day and because the forest feels so inviting, you venture further. As you go deeper into the forest you feel at one with the wildlife and nature around you.

As you stroll, deep in thought, you become aware of a presence by your side. You continue walking, and notice that the connection between you and your companion is very strong. You can feel that the energy of your companion is calm and serene, and also wise and full of love for you.

There is something familiar about your companion. Instinctively, you know this is your Future Self from a thousand years ahead. Before you is a clearing and together you make your way there.

When you reach the clearing you turn and face each other.

You take a moment to look at your Future Self. You smile at your Future Self because you know they are there to help you. They have come back from the future to guide you on your current path. Feel the warmth and love coming to you from your Future Self.

In your mind you can speak telepathically to your Future Self; ask them what they need to tell you. What guidance do they have for you?

Be aware of the energy you are receiving from your Future Self: a gentle but powerful energy that will heal your past. Allow yourself to absorb this healing energy.

What do you need to know? Ask your Future Self anything you wish.

Why has your Future Self come back to help you? Is there something you are meant to be doing? Maybe you have a special role or purpose to fulfil?

Now ask your Future Self what message they have for the world. What do the people of Earth need to know right now?

Take a moment to say goodbye to your Future Self and know you will be connecting to them again very soon.

Complete your journey by closing yourself down (see p. xxix–xxx).

Don't forget to write down your experience in your journal, before returning to your usual activities.

STRENGTHENING THE BOND WITH YOUR FUTURE SELF

Now that you have met and connected with your Future Self it is a good idea to strengthen that bond and build a greater link between you. There is a mutual benefit to this connection. Your Future Self needs your help in creating the right circumstances now to ensure their own future. They, in turn, will help you by guiding you along your life's journey. Although you are a great many years apart you can make a huge difference to each other.

This is actually a very simple process. After all, you are not trying to connect with an unknown being – this is yourself in the future. It would be hard to find a better guide to work with.

It is a good idea initially to make contact daily. Building your connection over time will make that connection stronger than if you rush in and try to do it all at once. It is a bit like getting to know a new friend; you bond bit by bit, getting to know more about each other, until you are firm buddies. The ideal timeframe would be to meet your Future Self every day for ten days, taking just ten minutes or so to strengthen the bond between you.

EXERCISE: TO STRENGTHEN THE BOND

Before starting Step One, spend a few moments opening up, following the instructions on p. xxix.

Step One: connecting with your Future Self

Find yourself a comfortable place to relax; somewhere where you will not be interrupted.

Sit quietly, close your eyes and focus on your breathing. Allow yourself to let go of all your current thoughts and just be aware of a feeling of peace.

Imagine you are back in the clearing in the forest where you first met your Future Self. Enjoy the peace of this beautiful place for a few minutes as you relax and breathe in the fresh forest air and listen to the sounds of nature.

Be aware that your Future Self has joined you and is now sitting opposite you. Sit quietly as you notice their presence. Spend a little while enjoying this moment.

Now focus on your aura, and sense it becoming bigger and brighter; allow it fully to shine outwards and be aware that your Future Self is doing exactly the same. Their aura is also becoming bigger and brighter and shining outwards; both auras are now shining brightly.

Notice that your Future Self is wrapping their aura around you and enveloping you.

Feel the warmth and love surrounding you. Your Future Self has nothing but pure, unconditional love for you. Now allow their aura to wrap around you, and yours to wrap around them. You are sending mutual loving energy to each other.

What messages come to you? Allow yourselves to connect and communicate.

When you are finished, bid farewell to your Future Self and know you will be meeting again soon.

Note: practise Step One every day for ten days to connect with your Future Self and feel the bond between you grow a little stronger each day. Allow your mind to flow as you connect with each other; you may find you are receiving messages from your Future Self.

Be aware of the change in your vibration; be aware of your new-found wisdom and your new awareness and attitude to life.

Step Two: blending energies

Note: please do not try Step Two until you have connected with your Future Self regularly for at least ten days. This is a powerful energy that you need to become accustomed to.

Step Two enables your energies to blend. Begin as in Step One, to the point when your Future Self has wrapped their etheric energy around you and yours is wrapped around them. Now allow both your auras to become bigger and brighter and spread outwards. Then, as you continue to wrap your auras around each other feel your auras blending together. Be aware of an exchange of energy.

Take time to connect with the new vibration, allowing this to happen naturally. You may wish to only blend a tiny bit at first: do what feels right to you. There is no rush; now that you have found each other you will stay connected.

When you are ready, visualise your auras returning to their usual size and brightness.

Practise Step Two for as long as you feel you need to, before moving on to Step Three.

Step Three: connecting your etheric cords

The final step is to create an etheric cord between you and your Future Self. You will know when you are ready to do this. You will have a sense of complete faith and trust in your Future Self. You will have read the instructions in Chapter 1 for cutting etheric energy cords: now you are ready to create a very special cord with your Future Self.

As you can imagine, your Future Self knows exactly how to do this. All you need to do is be ready to receive. Again, only do this when you are ready – there is no rush. Take each step only when you feel quite ready.

When the time feels right, tell your Future Self that you would like to connect with them by etheric energy cord.

Then sit quietly and be aware of the energy flowing back and forth between you. Be aware of a cord forming between you and becoming a vibrant force.

With this cord you and your Future Self will be connected at all times. You will be telepathically and energetically linked. Don't worry – it will not interfere with your everyday life. It will just mean that you have this powerful energy in the background, ready to call upon whenever you need to.

At this point you no longer need to make daily contact, though you can if you wish. Ideally, spend at least ten minutes a week connecting, just as you did at the beginning of the exercise, by going to the forest clearing and sitting opposite your Future Self.

During these meetings you can communicate with your Future Self and ask questions. You can also call upon them for protection if you feel worried or nervous. But do also allow a time to be silent and simply be aware of their connection with you. You will find these silent times very powerful, and you can allow their wisdom and energy to flow to you. Their advice and healing energy will invigorate you.

Your Future Self will gradually become your ultimate guide and perhaps even your best friend.

Note: remember to complete the exercise each time by closing yourself down (see p. xxix–xxx).

The conversations with my Future Self taught me that each decision we make can have many consequences, and that it is vital to find our true path. I was told that we too often allow our past to influence our present and control us; then, instead of making a strong new pathway, we keep re-treading the old ones, even though that is the last thing we want.

The key is to go back and create better pathways in your past. This will have an immediate effect on your present and so open up a better, more positive pathway to your future. How wonderful is it to know that you are about to take a better route? All you need to do is take a look at the future to see what outcomes you are not happy with, then go back into the past to fine-tune your decisions.

Throughout this book you will be doing many exercises to clear your past and build a better future. The Buggy exercise opposite is designed to help you with the finer details and will enable you to weigh up a number of options until you create exactly the outcome you want. Don't make the mistake of thinking that it's only important to make big changes in your past; fine-tuning is just as important, because without it you will continue to allow decisions you made in the past to hold you back. In Yvonne's story, following the exercise, there are some good examples of how she looked at different options until she found exactly the right one. You can use the Buggy to weigh up as many options as you wish.

It may be that your future already looks pretty rosy, but you are aware that it could be even better. This exercise will help you find that better option, even if you have already made a different choice. The Buggy exercise can create a wonderful change of circumstances for you *right now*! I especially like it for people who believe they are unlucky. Often, they simply need to 'tweak' their past and future to find that their 'luck' suddenly changes for the better.

The Buggy allows you to manoeuvre in different directions in time, backwards and forwards, so that you can try out different possibilities. It allows you to test as many paths as you wish in both your future and your past. You may prefer to have someone work with you to guide you and prompt you, ideally a qualified Future Life Practitioner (see Resources).

EXERCISE: THE BUGGY

Before you start, follow the instructions on p. xxix for opening yourself up.

You now find yourself sitting in a little buggy, much like the ones you see on a golf course.

Surrounding you is a vast, sweeping landscape with the greenest grass and deep, rolling hills. You notice there are many pathways in front of and behind you, and deep in your inner being you know these pathways will take you to different scenarios. They represent your life and the many pathways you can take and have already taken. With this Buggy you can roll forward and backwards, trying out as many different options as you wish.

First, take the path in front of you and roll forward three years. Get a sense of where you are and what you are doing. Are you happy with all that is going on? What areas could be better? Focus on the main area you wish to improve. Take time to focus on what you need to make this happen. What timeframe do you need to create that change?

Is there something you can change in your current time or do you need to roll backwards to a time in the past? Allow the answers to come to you, staying aware of what you would like to improve.

Remember, you can roll back as far in time as you wish. Allow your own instincts to guide you. Notice that ahead of and behind you there are many pathways; there are a great number of options and you can try out as many as you wish.

If you need to go back to the past, use the Buggy to roll back to whatever time is right for making those changes. Focus on what you would like to improve and use the Buggy to go back to the original incident or point of decision in your past. Go back to the earliest event connected to this issue.

If a recognisable time does not come to you, just imagine sitting in the Buggy and rolling back until you sense you are in the right place to create the change you need. The key is simply to take what comes to you.

Be aware of what time you have arrived at. Now give some thought to how things at that time could have been different. Be aware of what you could have done differently. What other options did you have? Find as many options as you wish and use your imagination to create different scenarios.

Come back to your present time and notice that there is now a pathway for each of the options. Roll down the first option and see what outcome that option leads to. Now come back to the present time and look down the next pathway, roll down and again see how this option turns out. Try each in turn until you find the pathway that gives you the best outcome.

Now strongly imagine that you have made the necessary changes in your past to achieve that best outcome, and be aware that things can be different right now. Use all your senses and imagine the details in high clarity and colour. Sense with your whole being that the changes have been made.

Now stop and focus on how this feels: be aware of any change in your energy. You may feel different, and you may become aware of the changes that taking this option will create in your current time.

Now use the Buggy to come back to the present, and as you roll back along the timeline focus on the changes you have created and how much more positive your present and your future will be. When you reach the present time, go forward again three years into the future, as you did at the start of your journey. How does your future look now that you have implanted those changes into your timeline?

Focus on your better future and be aware of whether there is anything else you sense needs changing or just tweaking.

Roll backwards and forwards as many times as you wish.

When you have completed the exercise and closed yourself down (see p. xxix–xxx), write down your discoveries in your journal.

You can repeat the Buggy Exercise as often as you like.

Yvonne's Story

Yvonne is one of my many readers from abroad; she emailed me from Portugal, where she lives, to ask for a session on Skype. She told me she was desperate to talk to me and couldn't wait until she next visited England.

At forty-five, she felt that life was passing her by. She told me, 'I feel as if I don't have much of a future. Nothing ever seems to improve for me; it's always just the same old, same old.'

Yvonne felt she lacked confidence with other people, and also wanted a better job. She told me she knew she was stopping herself from having the life she wanted but had no idea how to change things. She said, 'I seem so stuck. It's as if I freeze when there is a chance to stretch myself and do the things I would like to. The problem is, no matter how hard I try, the same things happen every time.'

I used the Buggy exercise and took Yvonne forward three years. She told me, 'Just as I thought. Nothing much has changed. If anything, things are worse.'

I instructed her to go back to the earliest event she could remember connected with her problem, telling her just to let whatever it was come to the surface. This is what she told me:

'I am remembering being in school, and we each had to run around the games pitch in turn. I was enjoying myself and glad it was my turn until a boy pointed at me and shouted, "Look at the way she runs!" He then did a mock run, kicking his heels up behind him. The other boys joined in, roaring with laughter over my "funny running". I could feel my face burning with embarrassment; even to this day the very thought of it horrifies me.'

I asked her, 'Now look back along your timeline, to the present day and see what comes to mind when you think about how it has affected you.'

'I never do any sport now, never. My friends all took part in a fun run for charity, but I refused. They thought I was being mean, but I just couldn't bring myself to run in front of other people. Oh – and dancing. I went to a friend's wedding; I was the only one of our group just sitting and watching. I hadn't thought about it before, but it is all connected.'

'Anything else?' I prompted.

'Well what comes to mind is – I hold myself back at work: I hate getting up in front of people because I can't bear being looked at. I've stayed in the same position for years because at the next level I would have to run some of the trainings and give presentations.' She added, 'Gosh, I had no idea that one incident had affected me so much!'

I explained how once we clear the original block the problem fades away. I took Yvonne back to the point of the incident with the boys taunting her. We needed to change the energy and discover how things could have been different on that day.

Once she'd reached that time I asked her, 'How could you have changed things?'

'Well, I could have stayed at home or refused to run, then I would have been saved the humiliation.'

'Okay,' I replied. 'But we can't do that every time we're faced with something difficult in our lives, so think how things could have been different. What other options did you have?'

'Well, I could have ignored him. Or I could have walked over and told him just what I thought of him. I could have complained to the teacher. Or I could have waited until it was his turn to run, and pointed at him!'

'Stop and focus on which would be the best way to handle it. Use the Buggy to try each suggestion. First, imagine you walked over and gave him a piece of your mind. How does that feel?'

'Good, in a funny way. He looks shocked. But somehow it doesn't feel like the way to handle things.'

'Now imagine just not bothering to turn up or run. How does that feel?'

'Not good, weak somehow, and I get the feeling I'd still have to handle it again another day.'

'Okay, now imagine you waited until he ran and you pointed and said something cruel.'

'Oh, no, I really don't like that! It doesn't feel right at all.'

'Now imagine you just ignored him and his friends. How does that feel?

'A bit weird, I don't like it; I can feel my cheeks burning.'

Yvonne buzzed back and forth in the Buggy, checking out each option. I went on: 'Allow yourself to find the best way you could have dealt with this.'

'I need to not care; that's all. They are a pretty stupid bunch anyway. Just shrug and not care. Wow – that feels good!'

'Run through this scene again and imagine ignoring them and just not caring. Run through the whole scene and let me know when you get to the end.'

After a few minutes she said, 'This is really odd, but I feel quite strong. The boys looked a little nervous because they could see I wasn't rattled by them. At the end I stopped and stared point blank at them, not in a threatening way – just to let them know I was aware of them, but not bothered. They all actually looked down and looked quite awkward.'

'Right, now use the Buggy to travel back up along your timeline, to your present time and beyond. Notice if there are any changes. What do you see?'

'Oh, this is great! I can see myself taking part in a fun run. And I have joined a tennis club – oh, and I am dancing. I never thought that would happen. I love this!' she laughed. 'In my future fun run I saw my main antagonist. He was looking quite out of shape and scruffy and standing on the sidelines. This time it was he who looked embarrassed. I smiled as I passed him.'

As Yvonne arrived back in her present time she said, 'You know I feel quite different now, somehow more confident and less worried about what others think about me.'

Yvonne sends me progress reports from time to time. She is now working at a far higher level and has joined a running club.

THE DOMINANT BLOCK

During one of my conversations with my Future Self I asked her, 'Where do we begin?' I now knew that most of us need to clear our pasts, but all too often there is more than one area of our lives that needs improving or even transforming.

Sometimes we cannot see the obvious because to us it is the norm. A pattern that has been with us all our lives – indeed, perhaps for many lifetimes – can blight our lives without us having a clue as to where we are going wrong.

My Future Self replied, 'Come, I will show you.'

She took me by the hand and I became aware of feeling lighter. We began to float upwards until soon I was looking down on myself. I could see myself sitting in the clearing.

'Tell yourself to stand up,' she instructed. As I did so I saw myself stand up, and at that moment many pathways appeared in front of me.

'These are the different pathways you can take in the future. Each one will be the result of a decision that you make. It looks confusing, right?'

As I looked down at what looked like the walkways you see at airports, I could only agree. The more I looked, the more paths I saw – some ran in straight lines, others zig-zagged; many of the pathways intertwined or overlapped.

'Now tell yourself to face the other way.' I did so and, as I watched myself turn to face the other way, many more path-ways appeared.

'This is your past. You see, there are just as many path-ways; these are what have influenced your life up until now. You are the result of all these pathways.'

At that point I didn't have any burning issues to resolve, but as I looked down I saw glimpses like snapshots of events that had happened in the past. They stretched back as far as the eye could see, certainly way before any current memories that I had.

I could see my parents, then my grandparents, then way back in my ancestry – all with the same problems and issues holding them back, generation after generation.

Then the major issue showed itself: a health problem. The lines ran right up to my present time, where I could see myself below. Looking at the snapshots of my past, I could see that many longstanding issues had been cleared: the energy lines petered out and no longer reached me. However, I could also see that there were still a few lines to clear. 'More work to do!' I sighed.

My Future Self read my look of dismay. I had worked hard to be healthy and truly believed I'd cleared all the links from my past connected with my health.

'Well done,' she said. 'Some people never clear anything; others clear a little, and others actually make things worse. Just know there is no one walking the Earth right now that doesn't have any links from the past. So don't worry, I am about to teach you how to clear the way very quickly.'

I then used the Three Passageways exercise (see p. 14–17) to identify and clear past negative health links from my ancestry, which I discovered were to do with overworking and poor eating patterns. As I cleared these past energies, my future became clearer.

You are now ready to do the same, to find the key issue that you need to deal with. You can discover it by using the following exercise. Often the dominant issue is not what we believe it to be, which is why this exercise is so important. It may be the case that the block is something we regard as normal, something we take for granted in our everyday life and are unaware of. It may well be the norm in our family or cultural background. The key is to allow it to come to you naturally.

Note: before you do this exercise, do make sure you have connected sufficiently with your Future Self and have completed each stage of the process.

EXERCISE: THE KEY ISSUE

Before starting, open yourself up following the instructions on p. xxix.

Now, go back to the clearing and sit facing your Future Self.

Take a few moments to connect with your Future Self and then tell them you wish to view your dominant issue: the issue that has held you back the most in your life.

Be aware that your Future Self has taken you by the hand as you float gently upwards until you are looking down on yourself sitting in the clearing.

As you float above the clearing, be aware of all that has happened to lead you to where you are today.

Look down and see yourself stand up; now see pathways appearing ahead of you – these are the pathways still to be taken. Now watch yourself turn around as more pathways appear, the pathways connected to the past.

Focus on the pathways. You may see them as paths or walkways, as I did, or perhaps as roads, or even lines or maybe streams of energy.

Notice which ones stand out that you sense are holding you back: which have the greatest hold on you? Which can you feel draining your energy? Take time to identify them. You can zoom in on them if you wish, as if you were using a camera with a telescopic lens.

Maybe some have come to the surface or have changed colour. As you look down, be aware of what thoughts, feelings and impressions come to you.

What is the common theme running through your pathways and how does this affect you right now? What is the dominant issue that is stopping you from having the future that you want?

Close yourself down at the end of the exercise, following the instructions on p. xxix–xxx.

Once you've identified the dominant issue – maybe love, wealth or health – you may go straight to the relevant chapter in this book and work on that issue. (In later chapters we will be fine-tuning and pinpointing key issues, and you will find a number of techniques to clear the way further and fast-track you to a better future.) Or you may prefer to work your way through the chapters in order. Do whatever feels right to you.

Sally's Story

Sally arrived at my office and spoke in an apologetic voice:

'I am probably just expecting too much from life. Nothing terrible has happened, yet I have a general feeling of being miserable for no reason; my life is just dull. It's as if there is something hanging over me that permeates every area of my life. Yet somehow I know this is not how things are meant to be. I see others having a great time and don't understand why so much is passing me by.'

I felt Sally needed to discover her key issue to find out what was dragging her down. In her own words she was 'a good person'. She put in a lot of effort, yet things never got any better. Now, approaching forty, she had decided enough was enough.

I took Sally to an overview of her timelines to discover if there was one dominant issue. As she looked down over the many pathways she said, 'I am not seeing anything. I just have a feeling of great sadness. Ah – now I can see my family; they are all pretty miserable too.'

'What is happening?' I asked her. 'Why are they miserable?'

'No real reason, nothing much is happening. That is how they are; for them the cup is always half empty.'

'Where does this attitude come from?'

'From here I can see it goes right back through our ancestry, but it seems to have got much worse, it has almost peaked with my parents, I have no idea why. We didn't have life on a plate, but it was not that bad either.

'It's as if they are in the habit of being negative. As I look down on my pathways I am remembering being a little girl around the age of eight. I came second in my class end-of-year test. My teacher praised me and I got to wear a big, shiny badge. I burst through the front door full of pride to tell my parents, only to be met with, "Only second and 85 per cent! You should have tried harder."

'I can see now how this attitude has seeped into everything. They almost wanted things to go wrong or something to moan about. I remember my father looking disappointed if the doctor gave him the all-clear. On holiday they would search the holiday flat until they found something they didn't like. It was as if they couldn't relax until they found that the bed was too hard or the sink was dirty.

'It was the same if we met new people; my mother would ask probing questions, trying to find a chink in their lives. Once she'd discovered a problem in their marriage or finances, she seemed to settle.

'We once met a wonderful family; they had a girl about my age and we became firm friends. Her family was happy and successful. My mother tried to find a chink, but this time she couldn't find one. Eventually, she insisted we "keep away from them, they are obviously hiding something". I can really see how this has affected my life.'

I asked her, 'Why has this become stronger in your recent family?'

She replied, 'Well, partly because they refuse to look at themselves, but also what you focus on you attract. Both my parents came from negative families. People always said they were well matched, and I can see why! Unfortunately, all they did was make each other worse.'

I worked with Sally to cut the negative cords. As she left my office she said, 'Let's see if I can teach them how to enjoy life a little more.'

———————————

Use the Key Issue exercise to discover your most dominant issue. The forthcoming chapters will show you exactly how to clear the way not only to a better future for yourself, but also for other people, the world and the universe.

CHAPTER 3

YOUR HEALTHIEST
POSSIBLE SELF

Could you be healthier, more vibrant and youthful? Do you suspect you have patterns that are not helpful to your health, such as poor eating, smoking or lack of exercise? Or maybe you have inherited health issues that have run through previous generations of your family, or which may even have come from a past life.

In this chapter I shall be looking at how our family histories affect our health, and suggesting ways of improving and maintaining your well-being. There isn't space to cover every health problem here, so I shall be focusing on issues stemming from the kind of habitual behaviours that you can actively take charge of. I shall also look at some of the problems relating specifically to the times we live in, such as eating disorders and addictions.

You will see from my clients' stories that once you have found the origin of your problem, using the Three Passageways (see p. 14–17), there are a number of ways in which you can re-write your past to create a healthier present. You can choose the most appropriate for your needs, including cord-cutting (see p. 26–7), re-visualising past events and looking at yourself in the future (see the Mirror Room exercise, p. 74–7).

My Future Self told me that health was the most important thing for us to look after, yet we place greater value on so many other things. She said: 'What can be more important than the health of your own body? You cannot change it when it wears out as you would a car. Yet many of you pay more attention to your cars and houses than to your health.'

She explained that through our lack of care we are creating sick bodies, which in turn create a sick world; but by simply making small changes to our lifestyles not only can we benefit ourselves: the world will benefit too.

'All it takes for the world and its people to be healthier and happier is to make tiny changes. Many of these new behaviours come from past patterning, so the first step is to look to your past and see what you have carried with you through time.'

Note: if you have a serious long-term condition, while you may find the exercises helpful, it is important to consult your doctor and follow any medical advice you have been given.

FAMILY HEALTH PROBLEMS

My own family, the Russells, had a tendency to suffer from stomach and digestive problems. Throughout my childhood I often saw my father take remedies; his mother died from bowel cancer, as did his brother, my uncle. You may not be surprised to learn that I also developed digestive problems, an irritable bowel and appendicitis, and like my father I took a host of remedies.

A few years ago I met up with one of my cousins, who mentioned that he had to be careful of his stomach because it was so easily upset. He added, 'It's the Russell stomach.' It was almost as if we were conditioned to have this problem.

Luckily, I cleared this health issue many years ago; it has never reappeared and fortunately has not been carried down to my children. We have broken the pattern.

The key with these family health problems is first to discover when and how they began and then how to clear them. My own issues came from my ancestry; I traced the 'Russell stomach' back many generations to a great-great-great-grandfather who died of an ulcerated stomach. His son was always being told he would follow in his father's footsteps. The family was actually talking about his career, but a much broader message became embedded within him. So faithfully did he follow in his father's footsteps that he died from an ulcerated stomach at exactly the same age. From then on, the pattern was set.

Some of my clients are already aware that their health problems are part of a family pattern, like Geraldine's.

Geraldine's Story

Geraldine knew before she came to see me that her problem ran in her family. She was not the easiest client to work with; she had very fixed ideas about what she would and wouldn't try. Still, I knew she was suffering and wanted to see if I could help.

Her arm had plagued her for years and after two operations on her tendons she was still in pain. Doctors had told her that the discomfort might ease in time, but that she would always have problems.

Geraldine was a cook in a school, so her arms were constantly in use. She told me, 'Every day I need to pick up large pots of food and mix ingredients by hand, and every single day I am in pain.' Bluntly, she added, 'I am not sure about all this stuff that you do, but I'm willing to try anything.'

I explained my work to Geraldine and that, often, such problems can be traced back to the past. There was no need to take her to the Three Passageways; she immediately told me, 'I can already tell you the answer to that one. All the women in my family have been cooks, and we've all had problems in our tendons. It goes way back in our history.'

I told her how we could help to clear some of that past energy. She replied, 'Oh, I've had counselling and all that stuff. I want to try something else now.' No amount of explanation would shift Geraldine. Fortunately, when I suggested we look at her alternative health futures she liked this idea and easily relaxed.

As she arrived at the first option her arm was still hurting, but had eased slightly. I asked her what she had done to make a difference. She replied, 'I am working fewer days, but now I am struggling for money. I will need to go back to full-time work which means the pain will return – but hey-ho!'

In the second option she'd had yet another operation, but there was no improvement. Geraldine sounded deflated as she said, 'More time off work, more hospital and no difference.'

However, in the third and best possible health future, Geraldine beamed as she reported her arm was completely free from pain. I asked her to look to see what had brought about her recovery.

She told me, 'I am lying on a bed having acupuncture. I am also aware that I have lost weight.'

'How did you lose the weight?' I asked.

'Just by following a healthy diet and cutting out the rubbish.'

Over the next few weeks Geraldine started seeing an acupuncturist and went on a healthy diet.

She called me to say, 'The pain is reducing almost by the day; in fact, I am now nearly pain-free. I won't be so sceptical in the future. This has stopped a lot of misery for me and given me a better future. Now I can work and pay my bills, and enjoy my life without pain. I may even take up badminton again!'

A HEALTHIER FUTURE

The effort to lead a healthy lifestyle is often put on hold because we will not see the benefits immediately. So young people continue to smoke because the future is unimaginably far ahead; or an overweight person tells themself a single muffin won't make a difference. But just suppose you had a snapshot, an image of how you will be in the future when you can see the results of your current decisions? Imagine that you could discover exactly what you need to do right now in order to improve your life in years to come?

The following exercise will show you the state of your health and well-being in ten years' time if you continue to follow your current patterns. You will then look at another, far healthier you and discover how that future can be created. You will gain some very real answers not only to improving your health but also to helping prevent potential future problems. As we all know, prevention is better than cure. Making the right decisions now will have a long-lasting effect for the future.

EXERCISE: THE MIRROR ROOM

Start by opening yourself up (see p. xxix).

Now, imagine you are standing at the beginning of a long white corridor. As you look down the corridor you can just about see a red door at the end.

Make your way down the corridor, and as you do so, think about your life and particularly your health and well-being. Focus on how you feel. Do you have any aches or pains? Are you stressed? Do you have any recurring ailments? Do you need to lose or gain weight? Is there anything you wish to improve? As you keep walking down the corridor, allow the answers to come to you. Do you have any ailments that are bothering you right now?

Keep walking and think about how you live your life and the things you do that may not be conducive to your health. Maybe you have little treats or do not exercise. Perhaps you have cravings or addictions to tobacco, alcohol or even tea, coffee or chocolate.

You are now approaching the red door at the end of the tunnel. Just know that on the other side of the door is a very special room. Inside this room are two mirrors that will help you to make big improvements to your future health.

The first mirror will show you how you will be in ten years' time if you carry on with your present patterns and lifestyle. The second mirror will show you your potential for health and well-being in ten years, and the changes you need to make in order for that to happen.

Open the door and step inside the room. Notice that the space is very minimal and feels like a sanctuary; there is a great sense of peace and calm. As you enter, you can feel a soothing vibration, a wonderful pulsating energy that vibrates through your whole body. Stop for a moment to enjoy the wonderful feeling.

Stand in the centre of the room and notice the two large round mirrors on either side of the far wall. Somehow, you know that the mirror on the left-hand side will show you your future self in ten years' time if you carry on with your present lifestyle. Walk towards it. As you approach the mirror you can see all the colours of the rainbow swirling and dancing in the glass.

Stand in front of the mirror and know you will soon be looking at your own reflection in ten years' time if you carry on with your present lifestyle and health choices.

As the colours begin to fade, the image of your future self gradually becomes clearer and clearer. Do you have more lines on your face? Is your hair colour different? Do you look older? Do you have any ailments? Or are you healthy and strong? Allow the answers to flow to you.

Be aware that this is how you will look. Stop, and allow the information to come to you. How do you sense your health is? Use your own energy to tap in to your future image. How do you feel? What is the main thing that you need to improve?

Know that there is room for improvement. You know that by this future time you can be both healthier and happier.

Now focus on what you can do differently *now*. What changes can you make in your current time that will make a big difference in ten years? Take time to allow the information to come to you.

Be aware of the day-to-day detail of what you could change right now that will make a big difference in the future. Is there something you need to start doing? Perhaps eating differently or taking up an exercise regime, or maybe giving something up?

Now focus on the one major thing that would make a huge difference to your future health.

Once you have gained the answers come back to the middle of the room. On the far right-hand side is the other circular mirror. You know this mirror will show you your best possible future health and well-being in ten years' time.

Walk up to this mirror; again, see the colours of the rainbow swirl and dance and again watch as they fade from the screen and the image of yourself in ten years' time appears. This time the image is of the healthiest possible you.

Do you look happy and relaxed? Are you glowing with health? What is the difference between the previous image and this one? What do you sense? Use your own energy to tap in to the information. How is your well-being? Is there any one thing that has made a big difference? Or is it a number of things? Have you made tiny changes to create this wonderful healthy future or is there one significant change? Take time to discover how you created this healthier future and what you need to do right now in order for this to happen.

Tap in to your future self, and notice how good this feels. Be aware of the positive energy and the wonderful feeling good health gives you.

As you focus on that feeling, be aware that the wonderful sensation of good health far outweighs that extra lie-in or cup of coffee, and realise how such tiny changes will create a strong, healthy, happy future you.

Close yourself down at the end of the exercise, following the instructions on p. xxix–xxx.

Vincent's Story

Vincent was not yet forty. He told me: 'Attending an old school reunion was the wake-up call I needed – although at the time I felt quite traumatised. I quickly realised that I had aged a lot more than most of my old school friends. I was also a lot heavier and a lot greyer.

'I've done well in life and truthfully expected everyone to be impressed with my flash car and successful company, but as I walked through the doors into my old school hall I could see the look of shock on their faces.

'After a few drinks my two oldest friends loosened up a bit, and one prodded my tummy and said, "I can see you've been eating well." The worst thing was he was a picture of health and fitness. He regularly attended the gym and was lean and tanned. Later one of the girls joked, "Your mum always fed your family a lot of stodge. I can see you've carried on the tradition." At school she was always catty, but still it stung.

'Later, I stopped and thought about my life, and how I sat at my desk all day, living on junk food. I thought I'd moved on from my family patterns, but instead of sitting in an armchair watching TV and eating rubbish I'd simply changed to a desk and office chair. The effects on me and my body were the same.

'The trouble is I've never known any different. I plan to change things, but just slip back into my old patterns which have been the same since I was a small child. I can't remember the last time I ate vegetables or salad.'

Vincent agreed to do the mirror exercise with me. As he viewed the first mirror he could see himself in ten years if he did nothing to change things. His face had a sallow hue and he'd put on even more weight. 'I seriously do not look too good,' he said.

I asked him to focus on what changes he could make. He smiled, 'Interesting how you guide me to the small changes. I have always felt overwhelmed with the gym or going on a diet, but I can see here that just taking a nice stroll a few times a week would make a big difference. And my secretary often offers to pick me up a salad for lunch. Hey, this is not too drastic at all.'

Next Vincent looked in the second mirror to view his healthier future.

'Wow, look at me! I've lost a few stone and my hair is less grey. I think I may have done something to help the colour, but nevertheless ...'

'How does your future self feel?' I asked him.

'More confident because I look better, I am eating better and I have more energy.' He gave a small gasp. 'And, gosh, I never expected this, but I now have a girlfriend. She makes sure I eat healthily. I met her through a rambling club – nothing drastic, just gentle walks in the countryside. She is a great girl. I can't wait to meet her!'

After this session, Vincent went on to make a series of small changes to his lifestyle. Later he told me, 'I have no doubt that these changes will extend my life by many years as well as giving me a greater quality of life. Thank you.'

WALKING BACK THROUGH TIME
TO A YOUNGER YOU

This exercise is useful if you have an age-related health issue, or perhaps simply want to rejuvenate yourself so as to feel and look younger. You will journey back to a time when you were younger and healthier, and then you will bring the younger energy back into your present time.

It is important that you think carefully about the timeframe that you wish to go back to. Make sure that you did not have any health issues at that time, so that you will only bring back life and health-enhancing energy.

Find a time when you were also happy. If you feel uncertain, then just keep in mind that you wish to go back to a healthy, younger age and allow your subconscious mind to guide you there. You may wish to go back to a time when your hearing or eyesight was better, or perhaps you were more agile and fitter. If you have a particular health issue, then focus on a time before you had this problem. Take time to stop and think about how you were at that time. What age were you?

EXERCISE: WALKING BACK TO A YOUNGER YOU

First open yourself up, following the instructions on p. xxix.

Now, imagine you are standing by a river on a beautifully sunny day; you sit down and dip your toes into the cool, clear water. Somehow, you know this river is special. This is the ever-flowing river of time. As you look to your right, you know this leads to your future and as you look to your left, this leads you to your past.

Stand up and walk along the river bank towards your past, and know that you are travelling back in time.

You feel the warmth of the sun as it shines down on you. You feel a soft breeze gently blowing your hair and making the nearby flowers dance. Walking along by the river you are aware of the people around you enjoying the warm day. You pass by a family having a picnic, as the mother takes sandwiches out of a hamper.

As you walk, you are aware of time and that you are travelling back into your past. You notice how the people you pass are dressed; you see some teenagers playing ball and are aware of their clothes and hairstyles.

As you carry on your journey, you are also aware that you are changing, you are becoming younger and younger. The further you walk along the riverside, the younger you become. You are walking back through time to the time that you chose to visit – the time where you would like to be right now. Perhaps you were pain-free or had a more youthful appearance; maybe you were free of a health problem.

You may be aware of walking with more ease, of your skin feeling fresher; maybe you feel lighter in weight and your hair is thicker. Focus on all the attributes you had in your younger days.

Soon you will be reaching the time in your past that you want to visit.

Walk a little further and know that now you have arrived at the appointed time. Remember how you felt back then and feel this fully. All the good feelings you had then come flooding back to you and only good feelings and energies will connect with you during this exercise. Maybe your mind seems clearer, perhaps you are less stressed. Allow this to happen naturally.

Now take time to absorb that energy. Feel yourself soak up that energy.

When you feel ready, walk back along the river bank to your present time, keeping that youthful, vibrant energy with you.

As you arrive back in your present time focus on how different you feel – more youthful and vibrant and full of healthy energy. And remember to close yourself down, according to the instructions on p. xxix–xxx.

MODERN PROBLEMS WITH ANCIENT ORIGINS

Today there is a new set of problems that need to be addressed. Addictions and eating disorders are a symptom of people searching for inner nourishment. The number of overweight people is now at crisis level, but unhealthy eating patterns and addictions do not feed the soul. The opposite is true: these people feel even emptier.

A MESSAGE FROM MY FUTURE SELF

If you look back through history you will see that most of our ancestors had it pretty tough, no matter where they lived in the world. They could not pop to the local shops to pick up something for dinner or turn on the taps to get clean, fresh water. The sheer physical labour needed just to put food on the table was beyond anything we can imagine today.

As in many parts of the Third World today, our Western ancestors were at the mercy of the elements; if their crops failed they could face starvation. Perhaps a plague or rats or insects would devour the food that was meant to support them for an entire winter. Even after a successful harvest they may have faced the threat of warring tribes or a greedy warlord taking their harvest from them. They had no healthcare service and medical help could be several days' travel away, if they were lucky, so sickness was a serious threat and many died young. Conditions like these are still affecting large numbers of people in the world.

As you can see from some of the stories in this chapter, present health problems may well stem from the difficulties experienced in past lives, which for most people were nasty, brutish and short. Sceptics often argue that people who believe in past lives always claim to have been someone like the Queen of Sheba, Napoleon or Cleopatra. In fact, studies like the one below show that this is not at all the case.

Science Investigates Reincarnation

In the 1960s, psychologist Dr Helen Wambach carried out a study with the objective of proving that the idea of reincarnation was ridiculous. In the study 1088 white, middle-class subjects were hypnotised and asked to regress to a former life. The majority were regressed successfully, and after they awoke from their hypnotic state were questioned in detail about the lives they had remembered.

The results shocked Dr Wambach; the information they gave corresponded with the historical facts of the periods they recalled with almost 100 per cent accuracy. Between 60 and 77 per cent of her interviewees recalled living at or below the poverty level, housed in poor and even primitive abodes. The majority were farmers who laboured every day in the fields. None of the participants recalled being a famous historical figure.

Dr Wambach went on to publish her findings in *Reliving Past Lives: The Evidence Under Hypnosis* and *Life Before Life.*

At times when we view our ancestral past or past-life selves it is easy to judge ourselves or our ancestors harshly, but we can have no real idea of the challenges people faced. Imagine not being able to feed your children. Imagine having your home burnt to the ground by enemies. Imagine watching a loved one in insufferable pain and not being able to call an ambulance. How would you feel? Guilty? Resentful? Angry?

These emotions can stay in our genes for many generations and unfortunately recreate the very same difficulties our ancestors experienced. Past-life patterns can be repeated over and over until we clear them.

Rebecca's Story

In her late forties, Rebecca works as a PA and is a regular client of mine. One day she telephoned asking for an urgent appointment. She said, 'I've come to the end of my tether. I've tried everything to clear whatever is blocking me from having a good life, but somehow it just doesn't shift.

'What really frightens me is that I am beginning to lose my spirituality; I am losing my faith. I am in constant pain with my neck and nothing seems to help. I want to provide for my family, but it is difficult for me to work. I feel the problem goes deeper than simple health,' she said. Then she added, 'I need to dig deep.'

I felt sad to hear Rebecca was losing her faith; she'd always been a very spiritual person, trusting the universe to provide for her and believing that what she gave out she would get back. I could hear she was not just in pain, but now doubted everything she'd ever believed in.

Rebecca knew she needed to find the source of her problem and the Three Passageways (see p. 14–17) was the ideal choice for our session. When she entered the cave she was immediately drawn to the past-life passageway, and as she made her way down it and the colour visibly drained from her face, I could see she was having a powerful reaction.

'I can feel something, but I can't see it; it feels strong, but I feel I can't look. I don't want to look.'

'That's okay,' I told her. 'Take your time. Just see what comes to you and detach from any emotion.'

Rebecca described seeing many tunnels veering off to the left and the right. Suddenly she was swamped with images, thoughts and feelings. She was aware of being a young monk dressed in red robes.

'I am pretty sure this is Tibet. I am a strong, self-assured young man. I have a real purpose to my life. Our leader is a wonderful man, he is so full of wisdom; he is kind and caring and never thinks of himself.'

She described how the younger monks looked up to the elder; he was known to be a great teacher, with the ability to bring out the best in everyone; under his leadership they always felt safe and strong.

Warring tribes from China had already attacked a number of monasteries. So far this one had been spared, but now a new breed of merciless raiders had arrived. Rebecca shuddered as she related the story. 'They wanted to take us over; they wanted us to revoke our beliefs. But our elder stood his ground; he stood in front of his young monks with squared shoulders and said, "We believe what we believe, that will never change."

'The raiders threatened to throw us all out and take over our monastery but our elder said: "We will not leave our home."

'I could see he fully expected them to back down; his faith was strong and he believed he had right on his side – this was all the protection they needed.'

Rebecca went on to describe their shock when the elder was knocked to the ground and beheaded in front of the young monks. She said, 'That memory is etched on my soul. Deep inside me are those memories and the terror and horror on the faces of the young monks.'

Several young monks were also killed; next to die was the monk who was Rebecca – and at that moment his faith vanished.

Often, when I am helping a client to clear their cords (see p. 26–7) I can actually see them. Rebecca had one heavy cord attached to her from that lifetime, almost like the huge, thick ropes attached to ships' anchors. Luckily, Rebecca sliced through it with ease; as she did so, she smiled, and the colour returned to her face.

As we worked in this way to clear the residue from that lifetime I explained that it is common to have a problem in the part of the body that was damaged in a past life – in this case, her neck. Now she no longer needed this problem. She then spent some time changing the terrible event by visualising a happier outcome in which the invaders moved on and never bothered the monks again.

When I last heard from Rebecca she was back at work and pain-free.

———————

EATING DISORDERS

Official figures from the Health and Social Care Information Centre (HSCIC) show that hospital admissions for eating disorders rose by 16 per cent in England from 2011 to 2012. Three-quarters of these admissions were related to anorexia nervosa, and children and young people account for most of them. Eating-disorders experts have said that the figures are 'just the tip of the iceberg'.

I have treated a number of people with eating disorders and in every case we have traced the original problem to a past life or ancestry. Many eating disorders are also a family pattern, but have their origins way back in time. By clearing the root cause people with eating disorders can begin to live life to the full and eat healthily.

Note: if you have an eating disorder that is seriously affecting your health, you should also consult your GP.

Lorraine's Story

Lorraine, a young worker in a care home, had a problem with eating. The food would literally get stuck in her throat, as if her body itself was refusing sustenance. She was painfully thin, pale and constantly tired. Her doctor found nothing physically wrong and referred her for counselling, but this changed nothing. There appeared to be simply no reason for her problem.

A friend of hers had heard about my work and suggested she make an appointment. Lorraine had little expectation that it would help, but was by now at the end of her tether and her family and friends were desperately worried about her.

I took her to the Three Passageways (see p. 14–17); without hesitation she chose the past-life passageway. As she entered, her first words were: 'I am hungry.' She spoke with a soft Irish lilt.

'What is happening?' I asked her. 'Why are you hungry?'

She replied, 'The men have to eat. They have to work the fields and hunt all day. It's hard work, they need their strength.' We had clearly gone a long way back in history. She went on: 'When they shoot birds we can eat, but people are hungry. The crops are failing, just like last year.'

I asked: 'When was the last time you ate?'

'Two days ago. The men must eat first, then the children, women come last. And my little one needs the food more, her chest is bad, I must keep her warm. The man on the hill said he would give me bones from his cow's carcass to make broth . . .'

'What is happening now?'

'I made the broth. My babies ate all the broth and now they are sleeping, but there was none left for me. I will wait another day.'

'Go forward in time to when your husband comes home,' I suggested.

Lorraine's face lit up, 'My husband is back. He has three fine birds for the stew, so now we can eat. He is ordering me to cook the food quickly, he is hungry too. But I have to wait until he has eaten before I can eat – oh, please God, let there be some left for me!'

After a pause, Lorraine made a gentle sobbing noise. 'He says I don't need to eat. He is telling me to sell the rest of the stew for whisky. I am now so weak – I know he will beat me, but I must eat.'

Lorraine described how she sat outside eating some of the stew when her husband found her and beat her; then he put his hand down her throat to make her throw up. At this point Lorraine felt the now familiar feeling of her throat closing up.

I explained to Lorraine that we needed to create a different past for her, one that was full of love, in which everyone had plenty to eat, and she readily agreed. I instructed her to go back again down the past-life passageway to the point she had reached before, but this time to see her husband bringing home plenty of food and being pleased to watch her happily cooking for the family. Lorraine imagined him smiling proudly as the children tucked into their food. She said, 'You know my little girl there looks far healthier and stronger.'

I then took her forward five years into her future from her present time. She exclaimed, 'Wow, I look really good! I have rosy cheeks and my clothes are not hanging off me.'

Afterwards she told me, 'This explains a lot! I have always been quite frightened of men and authority figures. I become very subservient and weak around them, even though my boss is very kindly.'

Lorraine called me a few weeks later to report that she was now eating normally and was positively glowing.

———————

As with Lorraine, many eating disorders stem from past lives or ancestry, when the person has suffered from starvation, but in Karl's case guilt played a major role.

Karl's Story

Karl was bulimic. I could see he was relieved to finally tell someone and unburden himself. He said, 'Can you believe this? I am a forty-five-year-old middle manager, but I regularly throw up after I've eaten. It's as if I can't bear to feel the food inside me. My wife thinks I am a quirky eater – she has no idea how many of her lovely meals end up down the toilet.'

Karl was keen to get to the cause of his problem and readily focused on the Three Passageways (see p. 14–17). There was an intense concentration about him as he chose the ancestral passageway. As he walked down it his voice faltered as he said, 'We took their food.' A shadow of sadness crossed his face.

'Whose food?' I asked.

'I am standing with my ancestors and we have raided the neighbouring village and taken their food. Our bellies are full and we are laughing. My own family will survive, but their children and old people will die.'

Karl shuddered as he recalled his ancestors living in the 1600s in a remote Danish town. One particularly bleak winter had left his family and neighbours starving. The next village had plenty of food because they had planned well and stored up provisions.

He told me, 'My family took their food; I feel so guilty.'

I asked him, 'But you personally didn't do this – why do you carry so much guilt?'

He said, 'Someone has to. That is how it is. Someone has to carry the burden of guilt.'

I asked Karl to think about what they could have done

differently. He said, 'They could have prepared more and made better provisions. They could have taken just some of their food. You know, I have the feeling they would have given my people enough to eat if only we'd asked.'

I instructed Karl to build an image changing the past events. 'Imagine your ancestors handling things differently, with everyone pulling together and surviving the harsh winter. Talk to your ancestors and advise them.'

Karl spent some time mentally working on changing the past energy by talking with his ancestors. Then he said: 'You know, I can see it never occurred to my ancestors to just ask their neighbours for help! They were used to taking what they wanted, that was how things were. But this is great: I can see the two villages working together, playing to their strengths and sharing what they have. Both communities will thrive as a result.'

As he left Karl said, 'I have always felt guilty if I have even a tiny bit more than someone else. Now I can see why.'

Then he added, 'I'm going to take my wife out for a slap-up meal! She often complains we never go out to eat. And I will pop some money each week into a charity box to help those with less than us. Now I can start to make some amends for my family's wrong-doings.'

Over-eating

Over-eating is an increasingly serious problem today. According to data published in 2013 by the HSCIC in the UK, there was a marked increase in obesity rates in Britain over the eight years between 1993 and 2011, with 24 per cent of men and 26 per cent of women being classified as obese. During 2011–12 there were 11,736 hospital admissions due to obesity (over 11 times higher than 2001–2) at an estimated cost to the NHS of £5.1 billion a year.

Like Sophia in the next story, many people today are simply eating too much, affecting both health and morale. Like Sophia, some go through years of counselling, slimming clubs and diets with little or no change. Often they put on even more weight each time a method fails.

Sophia's Story

Sophia told me, 'I am a binge eater. I am out of control around food; I just can't seem to stop. I actually do not know when I am full up. I try to eat sensibly and, God forbid, even diet – but once I get home at night I have this terrible compulsion to eat and eat. At times I can force down a whole loaf of bread or a huge cake. Then I hate myself, I really hate myself.'

She went on: 'I have tried absolutely everything; my counsellor says I am trying to feed something inside me. I have no idea what she is talking about. I need to find the root cause of this and I hear you are the person to speak to. I really want to clear this.'

I took Sophia to the Three Passageways (pp. 14–17) and, as I suspected, she was drawn to the past-life passageway. As she entered the passageway, her voice became gruff with a tinge of a Russian accent. She told me, 'I am a man, I am wearing animal fur. This is a very hard winter. It is especially cold and the animals we hunt have either gone to ground or have hibernated early.'

'So how do you manage?'

'At times we find a good piece of meat. Then we eat as much as we can; we eat and eat because we never know when we will eat next.'

Curious, I asked her, 'Can you not store the food in some way?'

'No, it will be taken from us – people are hungry. If we eat it, then it is in our bellies!' She laughed.

I asked Sophia if it was necessary for her to keep these patterns in her current life and whether they served any purpose. Her voice softened as she replied, 'No, not really.'

Sophia cut the cords connecting her to this past-life pattern (see p. 26–7) and as she did so she gave a big smile. 'It has gone, I know it has! I can feel it. I don't feel bad about myself any more.'

I wanted Sophia to fully feel how her life would be in the future, so I took her five years ahead to check how she would be. She told me, 'I am normal, and that is all I have ever wanted to be – normal. I eat normally, I look normal and, more to the point, I am at peace with myself.'

ADDICTIONS

I have always enjoyed working with addictions and have used FLP successfully with a large number of addicts. It is really satisfying to see people become liberated from harmful habits.

Addictions of all kinds are a growing social problem: from alcohol to chocolate, from computer games to porn, from drugs to gambling. At times it can almost be a badge that people wear with pride; recently I saw a woman wearing a

T-shirt emblazoned with 'I Am A Chocoholic'. One of my clients used to boast of his smoking consumption, announcing that he was a 'forty-a-day man'.

Addictions get in the way of our lives; they stop us from fulfilling our potential by keeping us locked into the addiction instead of living in the real world. We have ways of justifying such habits with statements like 'It relaxes me', 'It relieves my stress' and 'I work hard and deserve a little something'.

Addicts often see their addictions as a source of pleasure or comfort, but as my Future Self pointed out, they are seeking satisfaction in the wrong place; many people today are unknowingly trying to satisfy a spiritual hunger. Maggie's story, below, is a good example.

Maggie's Story

Maggie was in her forties; she came from a middle-class family and was the last person you'd expect to have a drug problem. 'My mother is a health nut,' she told me. 'She would freak if we took as much as an aspirin. She has no idea of my problem, none of my family has.'

Maggie told me how she'd gone straight on to hard drugs while at university. She was a model student with straight As, ambitious and well liked. But in her first month at college she fell in love with a senior lecturer, who introduced her to heroin. 'At the time it was heady and exciting, he was gorgeous and worldly wise, everyone adored him and many people envied me. The affair was partly me rebelling, partly trying to find myself and partly being in love with him and this new, exciting way of life.

'Of course, it all ended very badly. As the new students

arrived he found another young, sweet thing – apparently he does it every year. I was just another mug. And I was left devastated.

'But that was twenty years ago, and I am just as addicted as I was then, if not more so. Only now I am deeply ashamed. I've tried just about everything – rehab, drug counsellors, every alternative therapy you can think of and nothing seems to touch it. I really don't know what else to do or try, but you helped a friend of mine with a gambling addiction. So here I am.'

I took Maggie down the Three Passageways (see pp. 14–17) and she immediately went to the past-life route. As she walked down the lit passage she said, 'I can feel him, he is here.'

'Who?' I asked.

'*Him* – my lecturer, Tom. I've known him before, this is so strong! I can almost smell him.'

'What is happening, where are you?

'I am in Mexico ... He is a shaman. It is night time and very dark. We are in the desert, but surrounded by trees; it is like a haven in the desert. He is the chief shaman and I am his apprentice. This is such an important role: the knowledge has been handed down for generations, and he is teaching me. He is surrounded by students and chooses five each year to try the peyote. It is a great honour for them, and an even greater one for me to be his apprentice.'

Peyote is the cactus plant (used to make the drug mescaline), which produces hallucinogenic effects. In those times, in Mexico, it was believed that the experiences induced by taking peyote were very important for spiritual development.

Maggie explained that the preparation of the peyote was very complicated; from the growing and harvesting to the performance of the magical rites, the students would stand guard, nurturing the plant, even talking to it. Every single step of the way was steeped in ritual, and they talked about the cactus as if it was a person. Maggie said, 'No wonder he has such an effect on his students nowadays, if he was that powerful then.'

'How do you feel seeing this?' I asked.

'Well, I can see it had a place back then. It was a way to develop your spirituality and to be able to connect with the sacred, but in my current time I do that through meditation.'

'How do you feel about cutting your ties with this?'

'Oh please! I don't need a drug, even a natural one, to be a spiritual person.'

I asked Maggie to imagine that from that past life many cords were attached to her (see p. 21). When I asked her to find any that were negative, she found three: one that attached her to her lecturer, one that attached her to the desire for drugs and one connected to the belief that she needed a drug in order to be spiritual. 'Back then,' she said, 'they believed that no one reached a high level without it.'

Maggie walked back up the passageway and somehow I could feel a difference in her walk: it was steadier, less apologetic. Afterwards she told me: 'This addiction has ruined my finances, my health, my career and my relationships – I've been too ashamed to connect with anyone.'

A year later Maggie returned and I took her forward to a future lifetime. She said something a lot of people say to me: 'I feel I have wasted so much time. I have always wanted to develop my spiritual side and deep down I thought I needed a drug to get me there. I can see that this belief came from the past life, though I wasn't conscious of it at all! But now I know I don't need it – in fact, it was getting in the way of my spiritual side. I have found my true calling since, and I will be helping young students with addictions, depression and anything else that comes up for them.'

Tweaking Memories

Addicts respond to certain triggers or 'cues' based on past experience (such as needles or cigarettes) which connect taking drugs with feeling pleasure. But, according to a study published in *Science* magazine in 2012, 'tweaking' the memories of reformed drug addicts made them far less liable to relapse: scientists in China found that by changing the memories connected to the triggers they were able to greatly reduce any craving.

The researchers at Peking University 're-wrote' the original memories so that it would be as if the link between the cue and the craving never existed. The work relies on the idea that a memory can become malleable after it is accessed, creating a brief window during which it can be 're-written'.

ONLINE ADDICTS

Today there is a new wave of addictions, many of them connected to gambling and the internet. I am now used to parents telling me that their teenagers are living their lives through online games, in which they work their way up to a level where they can be a supreme warrior or a successful leader: they can be sexy and desirable – in fact, all the things they dream of, only without actually doing anything to achieve them.

Worried mother Hannah told me, 'My son plays violent online games non-stop. He never goes out or sees friends; he emerges pale-faced from his room to grab food to take back. I know he is up half the night playing games, and now his school work is suffering. At his age I was out with my friends and dating. I worry about his future because he has no social skills. Some days he actually smells because he hasn't showered; more recently he has become quite aggressive. I have no idea what to do.'

In online fantasy games you can hide from real life and its problems. Press a few buttons and 'life' will appear in front of you. Imagine what you might achieve if you put as much effort into your real life!

Janine, a university student, told me: 'My family and friends would never believe how I am in my online game. In the game I am so bold and fearless. I kill anyone who stands in my way, and I am sexy – other gamers admire me. In my everyday life I find it difficult to make eye contact with people; I find the real world hard to deal with. In the real world I am a plain nobody.'

There is no doubt that the internet has changed our lives, often for the good. However, the downside is that some people's lives happen almost totally in front of their computer screens; they even socialise online. Cases have been reported of people dying while playing non-stop for hours, sometimes days. Many of these were in the Far East, but in July 2011 British news media reported that a twenty-year-old from Sheffield died of deep-vein thrombosis after spending twelve hours at a time on his Xbox.

Internet Addiction Disorder (IAD)

A first groundbreaking paper on the topic ('Internet Addiction: The Emergence of a New Disorder') was presented in 1996 to the American Psychological Association by Dr Kimberly Young, who founded the Center for Internet Addiction in 1995. Her paper described a wide-ranging study covering online gaming, social media, online shopping, chat rooms and simply endlessly surfing websites.

Since then an increasing number of studies have been carried out all over the world, and treatment centres set up in a number of countries. In 2006 Stanford University School of Medicine carried out a nationwide telephone-based survey whose results suggested that at least one in eight (12.5 per cent) Americans was afflicted with some form of IAD (*CNS Spectrums: The International Journal of Neuropsychiatric Medicine*, October 2006).

The effects of internet addiction are both physical and psychological. Among the wide range of physical symptoms suffered by people who spend as many as thirty hours a week or more on the internet are carpal-tunnel syndrome, weight gain or loss, fatigue, strained vision and sleep deprivation. They also tend to have problems in their personal lives – with relationships, work, study and friendships suffering – and experience withdrawal symptoms when they try to stop.

In January 2011 the online scientific journal *PLOS ONE* published the findings of Chinese researchers who studied a group of young Chinese people aged between fourteen and twenty-one, comparing the brain scans of normal internet users to those of internet obsessives. Among the latter, they found changes in the areas of the brain responsible for decision-making, emotions and self-control, similar to those found in alcoholics and drug addicts.

Cyberporn

Online pornography addiction is another growing concern, with many young people having access to extreme images. On her centre's website Dr Kimberly Young writes that it is estimated that one in five internet addicts is engaged in some form of online sexual activity (primarily viewing cyberporn and/or engaging in cybersex). People who suffer from low self-esteem, a distorted body image, untreated sexual dysfunction or a prior sexual addiction are more at risk of developing cybersex/cyberporn addictions.

Experts are shocked at how quickly people who have never shown any previous sign of addiction become addicted to online sex. According to Dr Young, over 60 per cent of the clients at her centre, who wouldn't normally go to a strip club or rent an adult video, are downloading online pornography or talking with strangers in sexually explicit adult chat rooms. Jobs, marriages and other relationships suffer as a result. And there is always a risk of children coming across these websites.

Benny's Story

Benny described himself as 'naturally shy'. In his early thirties, he'd had the odd date, but had been single for most of his life. He told me, 'I find it hard to talk to girls. The whole dating thing is difficult unless you have heaps of confidence, which I don't. Now I think I have a bit of a problem. I spend all my time in chat rooms talking to strangers. People I will never meet. Every day I tell myself I will stay out of them, but every night I am back. I am now making mistakes at work because I am getting so little sleep.'

Benny told me how in the chat rooms he made friends and had got to know a couple of girls. 'The trouble is they live on the other side of the world, hence my lack of sleep. The time difference means I am sleeping odd hours. My boss has commented on how drained I look. I can't believe how I have let this take over my life.

'Then the other day I read a story in the paper about how many of the girls in the chat rooms are not genuine and are trying to reel in "sad little men" like me. Even so, I am there every night, just in case.'

Benny's lack of confidence needed to be cleared. I knew we could find a better outcome for him simply by looking at his future options, but first I wanted to see if there was anything from the past causing his low self-esteem, so I took him to the Three Passageways (see pp. 14–17).

I could tell Benny was determined to clear this problem. Standing in the middle of the cave he sounded very purposeful as he chose the past-life passageway. As he made his way down it, he said, 'I feel like hiding from people'.

'Why?'

'I don't know. I can't look at anyone, I am hiding my face.'

'Turn and face them,' I told him. 'This is past and cannot hurt you now.'

'They are laughing at me and pointing. Another person looks shocked and hurries away.'

'Why are they reacting like this?'

'I am not sure.'

'What is around you?'

'There is a house, we are by a lake.'

'Go and look in the lake and tell me what you see.'

Benny gasped. 'One side of my face is contorted; it looks as if I have been burnt. Yes – there was a fire when I was a baby, and now one side of my face is deformed. People don't understand; they are afraid of me.'

Benny went on to tell me how he'd hidden away and over the years had become more and more isolated. 'This explains why I prefer to sit at home talking to people who cannot see me. Sometimes my online friends suggest I get a webcam. I feel my stomach lurch whenever anyone suggests it.'

I explained to Benny that we could easily clear the past and release him from this issue.

Benny spent some time cutting the cords from the past life (see pp. 26–7). Once he was back in the cave I asked him to look at his reflection in a pool of water. 'Look at your face now, in your present time. How do you feel when you look at yourself?'

'I have a nice face! The fear of meeting new people has gone.'

There was still more work to do, however. I wanted Benny to see how his future could be so much better. Using the Buggy exercise (see pp. 55–7), I took Benny forward to see his choice of futures. In the first option, he was still sitting in front of his computer late at night. He said, 'As I expected, I was downgraded at work, so now I earn less money and the people online come and go. It is a pretty sad existence.'

I asked him to view another future in which he made the effort to meet new people. He told me: 'I've joined a social club. There are some really nice people here and I've made a few friends. Now I play badminton with a couple of chaps.'

Finally, I took Benny to his best possible future. I asked him, 'So how much time are you spending online in this option?'

He said, 'I don't have time for that, I am too busy with all my friends. I've met a great bunch of people and we go out every weekend.' He laughed. 'And I have a lovely girlfriend. I spend every minute I can with her. She is amazing.'

Curious to see how Benny would be still further down the road, I took him forward another five years, and there he was married with a child. He beamed from ear to ear as he said, 'To think I could have spent my whole life online instead of meeting the love of my life. Well – both of them, my wife and my daughter.'

It is easy to become obsessed by the internet and not realise just how much time we are spending each day in chat rooms, surfing the web or simply social networking. It's fine to spend a small amount of time online, but when it takes over your life it is time to find out what need it is fulfilling and how you can move forward to a more productive future.

LIBERATING YOURSELF FROM ADDICTION

If you have an addiction of any kind, you can use the following steps to help yourself:

1. Let your doctor know about your problem. He or she may want to monitor your progress.
2. Keep a written progress report – addictions can play

tricks with your mind. It is common for people to convince themselves they are doing better than they are.

3. Use the Three Passageways to determine the origin of your problem (see pp. 14–17).
4. Spend as long as you need clearing the issue by cutting any relevant cords (see pp. 26–7).
5. Now go forward and see your addiction-free future (see pp. 55–7). Take time to be aware of all the benefits and how wonderful it feels, and know that you are creating this wonderful new path in your present time.

Don't forget to consult your Future Self at any point to get the very best guidance with fine-tuning.

You may also find it helpful to join a self-help group focusing on your particular addiction, where you will receive ongoing support.

MOVING FORWARD

Whether you have a specific health problem or, like many people, feel just a bit below par, you know that you have choices, and that these choices affect your health. Every day you make decisions, some of them major – like adopting a whole new lifestyle – while others are tiny – whether to have sugar in your tea or an extra glass of wine. On one day you may decide to go for a run first thing; the next, you may choose not to get out of bed because it's chilly outside. Even decisions about who you mix with, how you spend your time and how you react to events will affect your health.

Most of our health habits are unconscious and come from our upbringing, including our environment and our family patterns. Rarely do we think about the long-term consequences of our health decisions; our small choices are not considered because the repercussions will not usually affect us for a long time. Yet sometimes all it takes is to make a few changes in order to create a far healthier future. The exercises in this chapter will help you to find out exactly what you need to do – and remember that at any time you can ask your Future Self for advice and guidance as to your next step.

CHAPTER 4

A LIFE FILLED WITH LOVE

Love is a precious gift that everyone deserves, but sadly it is something many people do not have. They wonder what is stopping them from finding true love. The answer is that just one thing blocks love and that is fear. People fear the pain that love can bring; but it is the pain that makes love all the more special.

Fear comes from the past and from what has gone before. Old wounds come to the surface — sometimes not our own, but wounds suffered by our ancestors or in our past existences. By clearing the past energy from old wounds you will allow love to flow freely.

A MESSAGE FROM MY FUTURE SELF

Love can bring you the best and worst times in your life. If you've ever been in love with a wonderful person who has loved you in return, you will know just how amazing and exciting each day becomes. Unfortunately, the opposite can also be the case, and many of the people who come to see me have a pattern of difficult relationships. Some have almost given up on meeting 'the one'. In this chapter you can learn how to clear these issues by creating a different past, and slip forward into a future filled with love.

Think back to a time when you had a conflict or were upset with someone close to you. Maybe someone left you with a broken heart, or perhaps you had a row with a sibling or close friend which you have never got over. As you remember the incident you will probably feel a wave of sadness or anger; you may feel distraught, even tearful.

Now, if you think back to times when your relationships have run smoothly, you will feel a glow of warmth and happiness. You will remember that life seemed easier and more contented. When you have good relationships all round, the world becomes a better place for you and for others.

Many of my clients come to me looking for their perfect partner. I would love to be able to produce one on the spot, but it is usually necessary first to look at what is preventing them from meeting their soul-mate. We learn about love through our families, and if there have been family problems in your current life or in your past life or ancestry, these may be creating blocks in your ability to give and receive love, which need to be cleared.

FAMILY RELATIONSHIPS

Most people have emotions they can't handle, so they 'screen them off', hiding them from others and even from themselves. They often choose partners with the same inhibitions, which are then passed on to their children ... from generation to generation.

From Families and How to Survive Them,
Robin Skynner and John Cleese

They say that you can choose your friends but not your family – the suggestion being that if you had a choice you would pick other people to be your relations, rather than those you have. I have seen several families torn apart by feuds. Money is a common cause, especially when someone passes on and leaves an inheritance; very often resentment arises when a family member believes they have not been given their fair share. Another frequent area of conflict is when several relations buy a house together or set up a joint business venture. When things go wrong, those concerned can get very angry, each party being convinced they are in the right no matter what has happened. All too often other members of the family are then expected to take sides.

Other family upsets occur when someone feels hurt or insulted. A client recently told me how her side of the family, including her ninety-five-year-old grandmother, was not invited to a family wedding. They'd been told it would be a small affair, but later learnt that several hundred people had attended; many of the guests did not even belong to the family, but were old work colleagues and even neighbours. The news soon spread among the uninvited members of the family who, not surprisingly, felt snubbed and insulted. Tempers ran high, and soon the entire family was involved. Things can get out of hand very quickly!

Often these issues can fester away beneath the surface for a long time, sometimes stretching back to past generations or even into past lives. However, these old rifts can be healed, using the exercise overleaf.

HEALING FAMILY RELATIONSHIPS

Each family has its own dynamics, patterns of behaviour and beliefs or attitudes that to them are the norm. In childhood, when you first make friends and get to know other families, you become aware of how different they are to your own. I remember one of my daughters coming home after having tea with a new friend and announcing, 'They have "afters" every single day, not just at weekends!' She was filled with awe at such a luxury.

Family patterns can be useful because they create boundaries for us to live within. Usually, all is well until something happens to change the status quo, such as a family member moving away or going to university, a marriage to someone from a different background or a career suddenly taking off, resulting in one family member having a higher income than the rest.

Most of us are not aware of our family patterns, since we have grown up regarding our families' behaviour as the norm. But when these patterns are negative – as with violence, addictions or prejudice – they can really hold us back. We may unconsciously stop progressing or moving towards what we truly want in case it upsets the others. Or we may adopt patterns of self-destruction and even self-sabotage, and then wonder why we never achieve what we want. Discovering and releasing these old negative patterns can transform all areas of our lives.

EXERCISE: THE ROAD TO A BETTER PAST –
HEALING FAMILY RELATIONSHIPS

First, as always, remember to open yourself up (see p. xxix). Next, go through the Three Passageways exercise (see pp. 14–17) to find out where your particular problem began – it may have started earlier than the incident that is troubling you now. Then follow these three steps to change the pattern in your present time.

Step One

In your mind, picture your family and think about all that has happened to create and prolong the problem. Be aware of your own emotions and put them to one side. If you have been personally affected or upset, imagine stepping out of yourself so that you can view your family as if you were an outside observer with no opinions.

Think back to your very earliest memory of this family conflict. Don't try to guess at it: just allow your subconscious mind to bring it to the fore. Your subconscious mind knows exactly where to look for the information.

Observe what happened without any blame or opinion. If you feel any emotions rising up, just let them float away and carry on observing. You do not need to experience any upset; this is simply an exercise in awareness.

Step Two

This step will create a different past for you, and a different vibration.

Imagine you are standing on a road which represents your life.

In front of you is your future and behind you is your past. Imagine turning round and walking back down the road, back through time, back to the past and right back to when this conflict first started.

Imagine you are now standing watching events unfold; perhaps the people concerned are complaining or maybe arguing. Watch for a few moments and notice how each family member reacts – they may be upset or angry. Someone may even be behaving smugly, as though they have triumphed over the others. Remain an observer and nothing more. Be aware of what these people are feeling and thinking.

Step Three

Now turn around and look up the road you have just travelled, towards your present time. Be aware that it has now divided, and there is a fork in the road immediately ahead of you.

The road to the right is the path you have just travelled along. To the left is a new road, one on which your family members have been free of conflict and have worked out tricky situations easily and without upset.

Do not allow any negative thoughts to get in the way – it is all too easy to allow that inner voice to take over and tell you, 'They will never change'. Remain detached and don't let anger or resentment temper your view. Take time to build up a picture of your family members treating each other well.

Now take a few steps along the road and see them going about their business and getting along fine.

Continue walking along the road, stopping every so often to see good relations between them all.

It is important to take your time; don't rush, but continue to build images of your family being in harmony as time moves on. Finish by visualising, at the end of the road, a family celebration with everyone enjoying a happy time together.

Now come back to your present time.

How do you feel? What has changed?

Finally, close yourself down as usual, following the instructions on pp. xxix–xxx.

Over the next few weeks and months look out for any changes in your family relationships and make a note of them in your journal. By changing the past you can change the present, and you will find various issues dissolving and patterns altering, so that suddenly your current pathway will become a lot more positive and easy. At the same time, changing yourself helps others to change, and you may well discover that your relationship with certain family members shifts as you see each other in a whole new light.

Kelly's Story

As far back as Kelly could remember her mother had had mental-health problems. Kelly told me, 'She would have terrible mood swings. When she was on one of her lows she would become quite cruel. She would humiliate me, sending me to school in dirty clothes, even though there were clean clothes in my wardrobe.

'As an adult I became overly defensive, and this affected my personal life. A relationship would begin, but soon I would become wary, almost waiting for the man to turn nasty as my mother used to.'

Using the above exercise, I took Kelly back down the path to the past to view her mother's behaviour objectively. She said, 'I know it is not her – it's as if something takes her over and she doesn't know what she is doing.'

As Kelly stood at the point of the earliest memory of her mother's cruel behaviour, I asked her to imagine that her mother had been kind and caring and free from mental-health problems. I then asked her to take the new fork in the road, to the left, and walk back up to her present time.

Kelly smiled as she described walking hand-in-hand with her mother. She was aware of time passing and herself growing up, but now things felt very different. She told me, 'I feel as if layers are being peeled from me. I feel somehow lighter as if a weight has been taken away.' Then she added, 'You know, in the end we were skipping along the road together, and there's me nearly forty years old!'

A few months later, Kelly called to tell me she'd met a charming man and they were getting along very well together. She said, 'He told me how we'd once met ten years before and he'd wanted to ask me out, but at the time he was terrified of me and thought I would turn him down flat. He said I seemed a lot more approachable now. Just to think, if I'd done this sooner we could have had another ten happy years together.'

PAST-LIFE CONNECTIONS

It is quite common for family members to have had close relationships with each other in previous lives which can affect their present lives quite powerfully. Just imagine if, in a previous lifetime, your mother had in fact been your daughter –

would that explain a few things about your relationship? I have seen many such scenarios, such as the woman who constantly fussed over her husband, who turned out to have been her sickly son in a previous life. Or the woman who felt suffocated by her partner, and learnt during a regression that he had been her jailer many centuries before.

One of the strangest examples I have come across was a father and son who came to one of my workshops.

The story of the father and son

As the delegates arrived at one of my FLP Practitioner Training courses I couldn't help noticing the elderly father and his middle-aged son, who entered the room together. They looked very alike, and were dressed similarly in sweaters and cords. They seemed embarrassed to be there and avoided eye contact with anyone. For the first day they spoke only to each other in hushed voices and when it came to practising various FLP scripts they worked solely with one another. During the training we swap people around for practising – a great way of gaining experience – but not these two! No matter how many times I proposed that people change partners they continued to sit closely together, still not engaging in the slightest with anyone else. It was as if the rest of us were invisible.

On the second day I gently suggested to the father that they might both wish to work with some of the other delegates. I wasn't prepared for the reaction: his face turned to thunder, while his son turned very red. Oops! I thought to myself. But then something interesting happened. The son whispered to his father, who nodded, albeit reluctantly, and they both went to work with other people. This was extraordinary, and I was fascinated. This particular session was to do with past-life regression and I was keen to see what would be uncovered.

After the practice session the father didn't want to speak about his experience. But the younger man returned to the group and I asked him to share what had happened. By this time the whole group was fascinated by the pair and intrigued to hear what he had to say.

He told us, 'My father and I were in China. We were con-joined twins. One day a surgeon heard about us and decided to take a look. He told our parents that we were not the worst case he had seen; he could easily separate us, and would waive his fee.'

Overjoyed, the twins' parents agreed and the children were duly separated. Everyone was happy except the twin who was, in this life, the father. Losing his conjoined brother made him feel lost and unsettled.

The son continued, 'I made new friends and even travelled to other towns and villages. My twin was left alone and became more and more withdrawn. Eventually, he became quite angry and resentful of my happiness. The odd thing was, as I re-lived that lifetime I felt as if something had stayed attached that should have left me when we separated, but during the session I felt it release and leave me. Does that make sense?' As he spoke, his father gazed at the floor, making no comment.

Later that day, we all looked ahead into our current futures and again the pair worked separately. As they returned, the son excitedly told everyone how he saw himself with a promotion which involved travelling abroad and meeting new people. He looked as if he had a new lease of life. The father, in the meantime, continued to look passively down, still saying nothing.

Six months later, however, I heard that while the son was off on his first business trip, the father had joined a bridge club and was making some friends of his own. Finally, they were building separate lives apart from each other.

WHEN CHILDREN BECOME A BURDEN

There is a powerful bond between parent and child. The parental instinct to protect one's child is natural and primal, and as the child grows, most parents will naturally help them to develop their own survival skills. In the early years they will teach the child to walk and feed themselves, and later how to read, write and gain life skills, so that when the time comes they will go out and make their own way in the world.

The transition into adulthood is marked in many societies with a rite of passage – a ritual to mark the time when they are ready to take on a more adult role. For the parent it is also a sign of letting go of the child and welcoming a new and different relationship with their offspring. Rites of passage vary from culture to culture and appear in most ancient civilisations; many are still practised today.

A rite of passage helps you to move from one stage in your life to another. Such transitions can be traumatic or frightening, but having a ritual of some kind acknowledges you and what you are becoming. It celebrates the changes you are going through and how far you have come. Usually there will be a support group to guide you and help you through to the next stage. The group may consist of wise elders or people who have simply been where you are right now.

In Africa, for example, many of these rituals include symbolic gestures and feats of endurance. In one African tribe girls are sent away at the onset of menstruation and taught about womanhood. In another tribe the girls are painted red and white, red to represent the life force and white for strength.

For boys the rituals are often to do with survival and strength. Some rituals involve cutting into the skin to identify they have 'passed' the initiation into adulthood. Others must lie among biting ants and not make a sound. In the Native American culture the young men go on a 'vision quest', typically spending four days and nights alone in nature.

Rites of Passage

French anthropologist Arnold van Gennep (1873–1957) coined the phrase 'Rites of Passage' and wrote the first definitive book on the subject, Les Rites de Passage in 1909. Van Gennep discovered that rites of passage comprise three ritual stages: separation, transition and reincorporation.

Today in the West rites of passage take the form of a twenty-first birthday party or being given the keys to a car, or a religious celebration such as Confirmation or Bar Mitzvah. Many major life transitions such as marriage, birth and death are also acknowledged with rituals, and these days Western women are even beginning to celebrate the onset of menopause as a rite of passage, for example with get-togethers discussing the positive aspects of becoming 'elders'. But we have fewer powerful rites of passage to adulthood than some other civilisations, and this can create problems.

There is a growing trend for adult children to continue living at home, whereas previous generations would go out into the world far earlier. Most parents naturally love their children, and continue to love them when they grow up. But when an adult child is still at home this can create a conflict for parents who would like to enjoy their own freedom – especially when the mother has to go on taking care of their needs. Although she may love her stay-at-home son or daughter, she doesn't love the extra cooking, housework and lack of privacy involved. Older relatives can find the situation very hard to understand.

Luke told me, 'Whenever I see my granddad he tells me how he was fighting in a war at my age. He thinks I should be out tilling the fields and bringing in the harvest. But the world has changed since his day.' Luke would not be able to pursue his law studies if he did not continue living with his parents. Other young adults – even young couples – are still at home because they can't afford to buy their own property.

Edward, a grandfather, told me, 'All my grandchildren live with their mother, who waits on them hand and foot. They say they cannot afford to move out but we used to live in bed-sits or shared flats. Today they all want their own flash apartment with all mod cons. In my day, once you started work you got your own place; that was how it worked. But they don't do that any more. I think they'll be there until their mother drops – and then some!'

Stay-at-Home Children

Figures from the Office for National Statistics show that in the UK in 2011, nearly 3 million adults aged between twenty and thirty-four were living with a parent or parents, an increase of almost half a million, or 20 per cent, since 1997.

THE BOOMERANG KIDS

The Boomerang Generation is a term applied to adult children who move back in with their parents after initially leaving home. Previous generations of parents have talked about 'empty-nest syndrome', the sense of loss they feel when their children leave home. This has made way for 'cluttered' or 'crowded-nest' syndrome, a term coined by Kathleen Shaputis in her book *The Crowded Nest Syndrome: Surviving the Return of Adult Children.*

This subject can be taboo. My clients almost whisper when they voice their frustration that their adult children are living at home. It's a problem: they still love their children, but their own lives are suffering. On the other side of the coin, young adults tell me they are filled with dread when circumstances force them to move back in with their parents. They fear they will be stuck there, either because their finances don't improve or because their parents may become infirm and dependent. And once back in the nest, it can be hard to go back out into the real world.

One very effective solution to the problem is cord-cutting – this will improve life not only for the overburdened parents, but also for their child, since it frees them both. Before cutting the cords between you and your adult child, re-read the cord-cutting exercise on pp. 26–7, as well as the tips below.

TIPS FOR CORD-CUTTING BETWEEN PARENT AND CHILD

- Take time to be aware of all the cords. There can be many between a parent and child, stemming from the moment of conception right up to the present day. The cords will represent different emotions: the immense bond between you, the milestones throughout your life together and all the different aspects of your relationship. You may have cords for friendship or neediness, security or even resentment.

- Once you have found the cords and identified what they represent, follow your intuition in choosing which cords to cut first. In fact, you may not be ready to release all the cords in one session, and may prefer to do it in stages. You can come back to the exercise as many times as you wish.

- Each time you do the exercise, first identify the cord you most need to cut, and when you are ready, use your laser-like scissors to cut it. As you release the old negative cords you release negative energy with them, and so healthier cords may form if you wish them to, and you will find that your relationship takes on a new and healthier balance.

Marjorie's Story

Marjorie had been emailing me weekly enquiring when my next 'Clear the Way' workshop was going to be and was clearly very keen to attend one. So when she did, I was surprised to see her sitting on the sidelines during many of the exercises. When I went over and spoke to her, she said, 'I know I've pestered you for this workshop, but now it's here I feel really nervous.'

She opened up and told me her story. 'You were talking about cutting ties with family members. Well, my forty-year-old son still lives at home with me. He moved back after university and I thought this would be temporary, but he has never moved out. I know I should encourage him to get a life, but I find it hard to let go of him – and Jake lacks the confidence to go out in the world.'

Marjorie described how she cooked and cleaned for him and did his laundry. They had got into the habit of sitting and watching television together every night – Jake rarely went out. 'I know it's not healthy to live this way,' she said. 'I've been single now for over twenty years and would love to have a relationship. I should be getting on with my own life now. But in a way we have a comfortable balance. If we changed things, we'd both have to take chances and get out of our comfort zone.'

I suggested Marjorie come for a private session so that we could work on this in stages. I explained that she need not do anything drastic like throwing her son out; she could take tiny steps that she was comfortable with. The beauty of cord-cutting is that you can work at a pace you are happy with.

As I took her through the process, Marjorie easily sensed the cords attached to her, and almost slumped forward: the sheer weight of them was dragging her down. She described envisioning a huge mass of entangled cords between herself and her son. I asked her to spend a little time focusing on the cords and noticing how they felt, and which ones were draining her. Then I asked her which cord she was ready to release.

'This one,' she said pointing to her lower abdomen. Once my clients start exploring their feelings in this way, they usually know instinctively where the crucial cords are and what they mean.

'What does it represent to you?' I asked.

'The carer.'

'What will be different if you cut this cord?'

'I feel it means I will be less hands-on, allowing him to take care of himself more, and this will give me more freedom.'

I instructed Marjorie to get ready to cut the cord. She hesitated and said, 'It's very hard to suddenly announce you are stopping doing something for someone that you have always done. It feels like I am rejecting him.'

I explained that she needed to start somewhere, and suggested that one night a week she should go out instead of sitting at home. Jake could have an evening to himself and prepare his own dinner.

She said, 'I can see I've been afraid of being left on my own, but the longer this goes on the less likely he is to make a life for himself. I'd love him to go out and enjoy himself.'

As Marjorie cut through the cord she gave a big sigh of relief.

A few weeks later she called me with an update. She'd chosen to use her free evening to go to a yoga class. At first it felt strange, but soon she was enjoying meeting new people and sharing a glass of wine afterwards at the sports centre's bar.

The difference in Marjorie was astounding. At the start, she had spoken in a slow, flat voice; now she was animated and excited. But when I asked how Jake was doing, her voice dropped. He was sitting at home watching television on his own.

'Don't worry,' I told her. 'Cord-cutting will change that. Just wait and see.'

Marjorie had no idea that while she was out, Jake was spending time online tracking down old friends. At school he'd been a keen rugby player, and shortly afterwards she learnt he had arranged a reunion with his old rugby pals. The last I heard from her was that they had both had to make dates in their diaries to catch up with each other.

BEREAVEMENT

It is inevitable that at some point we will lose someone, almost certainly a grandparent or parent, perhaps a partner or, at worst, a child. But until it actually happens it is difficult to understand just how devastating bereavement can be.

Of course, it is normal to grieve and this takes time – usually far longer than most people realise. One of my best friends, who had been widowed for some time, told me, 'It was four years before my first thought each morning wasn't about my late husband.'

Sometimes the grief is overwhelming. Losing someone who has been around you for your entire life, or who is the love of your life, is hard to get over. For many it is difficult to move forward when faced with an empty space that nothing seems able to fill. It is the finality of death that makes it so difficult: the thought that the person has gone and you will never see them again.

One of the most rewarding aspects of my work is helping people come to terms with the loss of a loved one. It can be beneficial for people who are suffering after a bereavement to take themselves into the future, to a point where they have moved beyond the period of grieving and have rebuilt their lives, but still retain the loving memory of the person they have lost. It also helps to keep in touch with and receive guidance from their Future Self; many of my grieving clients have found this really valuable.

It is becoming increasingly accepted that we all live many lives, and most of my clients accept this easily. When the bond has been especially strong you can be sure that you've had many lifetimes together; the good news is that you still have a number of lifetimes to come.

I've taken many people into their future lives to see for themselves that they will be reunited with their loved one. The relief and happiness they experience as they realise they will meet again one day helps them to move forward in their current time.

Take Eddy, for instance: his daughter is one of my long-term clients, and brought him to see me because he was finding it hard to get over the death of his wife. He had lost his beloved Lindsey two years earlier, but his grief was still just as painful. After his session he was a different man. He said, 'I actually saw her and spoke to her; I saw us in another future together. I feel I can let go now, knowing that I still have much to do here and she will be waiting for me until the time is right.'

I often give FLP workshops for businesses, during which people look at their work in future lifetimes to help improve their current business practices (see p. 155). After one of these, a young woman came up to me with tears streaming down her face. She told me how several years ago she'd lost her teenage brother to cancer. She had watched him fade away. 'Until now the only images in my mind were of him frail and in pain. Even when I look at photographs I still cannot imagine him before he got sick.'

Eileen then told me, 'As I looked closely at my work in my future lifetime I suddenly realised he was there working alongside me! I just knew we were brother and sister once again.' Her face lit up as she said, 'He was glowing with health; he looked so strong – just as he did when he was a child. I've struggled with my memories of him, but now I have a wonderful image in my mind of him in the future, leading the life he should have led. I could even see the mischievous twinkle in his eye that he used to have as a little boy.'

Later Eileen came to see me for a private session to reinforce the image. This time we looked further ahead in their next life, when she saw their latter years. She exclaimed, 'Oh goodness, there we are, two old people watching our grandchildren playing together!' She added, 'I can't wait to tell my mother. She has been very sad that he'd never had the chance to marry and have children. I caught a glimpse of her future lifetime too; she will be with her beloved son once again, and his children.'

Bereavement is particularly devastating when a partner is snatched away in their youth, particularly if there is some question as to whether their death was intentional, as in Bridget's case, below. Suicide is one of the toughest areas to deal with. Often those left behind suffer feelings of guilt or anger. Sometimes there have been no previous warning signs, leaving the bereaved person with a huge uncertainty as to what went wrong and why.

Bridget and Neil's Story

Bridget came to see me after losing her boyfriend, whom she described as her 'soul-mate'. She told me, 'I thought we'd be together for ever. I just cannot believe he has gone.'

Bridget and Neil had a passionate but volatile relationship – they often joked that making up after a quarrel made it worth it. On this particular night they had a huge row, and Neil stormed out, got on his motorbike and roared off furiously into the distance. The next thing Bridget knew, there was a policeman on her doorstep telling her Neil had died in a crash.

'It felt like he'd only been gone a few minutes. How was that possible?'

Neighbours had heard them rowing and soon people were speculating that Neil had committed suicide – that Bridget had driven him to it. Bridget herself began to wonder if indeed he'd crashed on purpose, and she spent every waking moment tortured by the thought that she was responsible. To make matters worse, some people turned against her, letting her know they thought she was to blame.

She told me, 'I have a handful of friends left and they tell me that it was an accident; he was a happy-go-lucky person who simply wouldn't do such a thing. But then I wonder, did our row make him reckless? I said some horrible things to him.'

The inquest found that the cause of death was accidental. The roads were icy that night and Neil was speeding. His family commented that he was normally a careful rider and never drove too fast. They also mentioned that they believed his mind was distracted because he was upset.

So Bridget had to deal not only with losing the love of her life, but also with the guilt of feeling she had caused his death. Over and over she said, 'If only we hadn't rowed that night.'

Bridget had frequently laughed about how they'd known each other in a past life, but somehow she had never thought about future lifetimes. When I talked to her about Future Life Progression, she told me, 'I've not heard of FLP before, but it makes sense. I just know we've been together before; when we met it was as if I recognised him. It was like being reunited and finding the other part of me. I often joked that we were joined by an invisible piece of elastic. So it makes sense we will be together again one day.'

I took Bridget into the future and as she arrived in her next lifetime she was immediately aware of Neil waiting for her. She cried softly and said, 'These are tears of happiness! I can see him and even touch and talk to him.'

I left her in silence to spend time with Neil. After ten minutes she nodded to let me know she was ready to come back. She said, 'He hugged me and said sorry for leaving me to deal with so much. He said that night he hit a patch of ice. He was angry and upset and not concentrating properly.' Neil told Bridget that they would be together again, but it was his destiny to leave this lifetime early; someone new would be coming into Bridget's life and she would have two children. He said that he would watch over her and her children.

His parting words to her were, 'Until next time, my love.'

CLEARING THE PAST TO MAKE WAY FOR LOVE

It is tragic to think that your perfect partner is out there somewhere and cannot find you, and you cannot find them. Everyone needs love and companionship and when we achieve a wonderful relationship we encourage others to have the same; we create a happy and loving environment for those close to us.

Before finding 'the one', most people have something to clear from their ancestry, past lives or childhood. We need to find the source of any problematic issues before we can create the right vibration to meet our perfect partner. Blocks can come from our family patterns or back in our ancestry, patterns of arguments, upsets and even abuse. We may be repeating patterns from our past lives which need to be resolved. Frequently, these blocks begin in childhood, when cold or unloving parents give a child a feeling of unworthiness. These blocks can be healed by clearing old energies and creating a different past in which the child was loved and validated.

The Cords of Love

Love creates strong cords, and once you bring sex into the mix you create the most powerful cords of all. Part of your own *kundalini* energy (this lies at the base of the spine and is sometimes known as the sleeping serpent; once it is awakened a higher spiritual level, even enlightenment, can be reached) goes into the cord which entwines with the other person's. Sex without love rarely includes this, which is why people feel 'empty' after meaningless sex.

Anyone who has experienced a powerful loving and sexual relationship will know what I am talking about. Sex addicts long for this energy, not knowing necessarily that this is what they are missing; they seek it more and more, as if the search itself feeds them in some way. Sadly, however, they seek it in the wrong places. Many search for sex with strangers, or experiment with increasingly kinky experiences, when what they are looking for can only be found via the *kundalini* energy that comes when sex is accompanied by love.

Sometimes this powerful *kundalini* energy flows mainly one way, and once the relationship ends the receiver can find it very hard to move on. Because their own feelings have been so powerful they can't believe the other person doesn't feel the same. When this happens the cords are still attached to both partners; that special energy is still there, albeit sometimes flowing only one way.

PAST-LIFE DIFFICULTIES

Sometimes, meeting your soul-mate brings up echoes of past lives when times have been unhappy. This is when fear kicks in and a negative energy is created. You may not be conscious of the cause, but wonderful relationships can soon start to go downhill when these old wounds resurface. This was the case with Sonia.

Sonia's Story

Sonia is a teacher in her thirties. When I met her, she was distraught at having recently lost the love of her life. She told me: 'As soon as I met Pete I knew he was the one for me; he was my man. I knew what he was about to say before he said it. I knew what food he liked. I could feel when he'd had a bad day and knew what he would need when he came home. But deep down, I always had a terrible fear in my stomach. It was a nasty twist, a fear that one day he wouldn't come home – that he would cruelly leave me and never return.

'I've never been clingy or insecure before. I put it down to the fact that I'd never been so in love, but this was out of character. One of my friends took me aside and asked me why I was becoming so pathetic. The worst thing was that I could see Pete was feeling pressured. Then one day he walked in through the front door and I could see in his eyes he simply didn't want to be there.

'I wanted to put this down to something else, but deep down I knew I'd driven him away with my constant insecurities. Pete left shortly afterwards.'

After discussing the situation with me, Sonia decided to

have a past-life session to see if she could uncover the root of the problem. I could see that she was nervous, but she was so keen to resolve her problem that she willingly followed my instructions and easily slipped into a past life.

Sonia told me she was living 'an idyllic life' on a farm, and described how she was smiling as she milked a cow. She was expected to marry a local lad; she was fond of him and he was a good person.

One day a troop of soldiers passed through her valley and set up a post near by. A young private was sent to Sonia's farm to buy milk and eggs. As soon as she saw him her heart leapt; he was so handsome and dashing in his uniform. As he approached her he took her hand and planted a kiss on it. Nothing like that had ever happened to her before: she was smitten.

The soldiers were stationed near her village for three weeks while they waited for orders, and during that time Sonia and the young soldier became close. Soon she had turned her back on the local lad and was head over heels in love with her soldier.

One morning she woke to see the troops packing to leave. Where was her sweetheart? Why hadn't he come to see her to take her with him as he'd promised?

She ran down to the camp to look for him. Several of the soldiers laughed and pointed to a nearby tent; inside was her soldier. Sonia was shocked to see that he was about to leave without even speaking to her. At that moment she realised he didn't love her at all – she'd just been a bit of fun. Humiliated, she walked back to her farm, aware of the villagers talking about her. She was so overcome with shame she threw herself into a river.

The young soldier who had deserted her was Pete.

As we discussed her experience, Sonia said, 'I have this real fear that he doesn't really love me this time around, even though I know that he does. I can see that in the past life he was young and about to go to war, but he did care for me.'

Sonia agreed to leave her insecurities where they belonged: in the past. She spent a few minutes cutting the negative energy cords to that past-life experience (see pp. 26–7), and as she cut the final cords a wave of relief swept over her.

Later, she sent a message to Pete asking to meet him, and they talked throughout the night. At first Pete couldn't see what the problem was. He'd always lived a bohemian life – he'd been a roadie with a band and usually moved home every couple of years. Most of his relationships had also lasted just a year or less.

Once Sonia told him about her past-life experience he understood that in his present life he was creating a similar pattern to his life as a soldier, never staying long in one place. He had no doubt that he loved Sonia, but until now he hadn't understood her insecurities. Later he said, 'Now I can see why this would trigger a reaction in Sonia! My past life was about constantly being on the move, but at my age I think it is time to put down some roots and give Sonia a more settled life.'

People often re-live patterns that originated in a previous life, which can be complicated to unravel. But learning what has gone before can give us great insight into our present behaviour and reactions, and allow us to correct them.

HOW OUR ANCESTORS AFFECT
OUR SEARCH FOR LOVE

My clients are often aware of their patterns: they tell me that they continually attract a certain type of partner – maybe someone who needs mothering, is controlling or has anger problems or addictions. Commonly, these clients have had a parent with similar problems and understand that this is where their own patterns stem from, though they still need help to clear them. However, not everyone realises how far back the roots of these patterns can lie. In Cathy's case the problem was a long-standing ancestral one.

Cathy's Story

Cathy's childhood had been difficult; her family carried a pattern of anger and violence. Her father and brother were both angry men and her mother would swing between being a passive victim and bouts of aggression, when she would fight with anyone unlucky enough to cross her path.

Over the years Cathy had noticed how she attracted men with similar patterns of anger and had seen a number of therapists. Determined to break the victim/aggressor patterns, she moved away and broke all ties with her family.

She loved her new home, and soon after moving in she met 'a lovely chap'. For the first time in her life she wasn't on edge. Everything was perfect until her boyfriend moved in, when his behaviour changed alarmingly. He would fly into rages at the most trivial things. She said, 'I feel like I am right back where I started! He was lovely when we first met; I am wondering if I have done anything to make him like this.'

It is not unusual for people living out victim/aggressor patterns to blame themselves for their partner's reactions. I explained to Cathy that by thinking in this way she was falling back into victim mode; her first step to free herself was to refuse to take responsibility for her partner's behaviour.

Cathy was despondent that after all her work on herself she was still faced with the same old issues. I had a feeling these went back further than her immediate family, so I asked about her grandparents. She assured me they were lovely and kind; the problem had begun with her dad and brother. However, I still felt we needed to dig a little deeper, so I took Cathy through the Three Passageways exercise (see pp. 14–17).

To Cathy's surprise, she found herself drawn to the ancestral passageway. As she moved down it she discovered that her great-grandparents on her father's side had been violent people. In fact, her great-grandfather had led a group of vigilantes to kill a man accused by a mother of murdering her child. Later the child was found alive and well; her mother had accused the man falsely because she had a grudge against him, while actually keeping her daughter hidden away.

Cathy's great-grandfather spent the rest of his life living in shame and depression.

This was never spoken about, and Cathy's grandparents reacted to the terrible events by becoming the opposite of violent: they were caring, understanding people who, throughout Cathy's upbringing, had shown no sign of the family's anger patterns.

Cathy travelled back in time to meet her great-grandfather, a big, proud and honourable man. She could see that he'd done what he believed to be right at the time, but he was mortified that he had taken an innocent life. Although those who knew well understood his motives and respected him, he could not forgive himself.

Cathy hugged him and told him that she understood. Next, she discussed with him what he could have done differently. After some thought he said he should have waited until he had proof, but had feared that another child would die if he didn't act. He had wanted to rid the world of what he believed was a monster. He realised now that he and his friends should have taken the appropriate route by contacting the local authorities. Taking the law into their own hands had been totally wrong.

Cathy asked him how things could have been different afterwards. He said, 'I could have helped to look after the poor man's family instead of wallowing in my own guilt and misery.'

Cathy then showed him a new, alternative pathway where this had actually happened. And, as they walked hand-in-hand along this pathway, the pressure lifted from him. He felt released.

Soon after her session with me, Cathy bumped into a relative of her boyfriend, who warned her that he'd been aggressive and bullying towards his previous partner. Shortly afterwards, she left him. Having changed her ancestral past, she was now free of the energy that had drawn her to bullies.

As often happens in such cases, the shift in Cathy impacted on the rest of the family. Changing deep-rooted problems in ourselves can unconsciously bring about changes in the people with whom we have close links. The next time she visited them there was something different in the air; her brother seemed to keep himself busier, while her father seemed more relaxed and less inclined to flare up over trivial things. And her mother had a freshness about her. Gradually, over time, the family home became far more harmonious.

Cathy also began to see her family through more positive eyes, and recognised that they had some great qualities; deep down they were caring people who liked to help others and to live a respectable life.

FINDING YOUR PERFECT PARTNER

I've been asked countless times, 'When will I meet "the one"?' or 'Will I meet my soul-mate?' A great many people spend their lives looking for their 'other half', their perfect partner, but in reality, meeting our ideal partner can be difficult and they may be anything but perfect.

In fact, it seems harder today than ever before to find someone special to spend your life with, and by looking for our soul-mate we put immense pressure on any prospective relationship. We expect the other person to be faultless in every detail and that only they will make us feel complete.

Our Missing Half

In his *Symposium*, the Greek philosopher Plato relates a speech by the comic playwright Aristophanes in which he describes how people were once androgynous – both male and female – with four arms and four legs and both sets of genitals. They led a wonderful life and had a great amount of freedom, but one day they decided climb to heaven and kill the gods.

▶

> When the gods got wind of their plans, at first they thought to kill them. Then they decided, however, to teach them a lesson and chopped them in half, separating the male and female. Thus they would spend their lives forever searching for their 'other half' to make them complete.

Often, when a person does meet their ideal partner they don't immediately recognise them – he or she may be completely different from what they expected. Thinking in terms of a soul-mate creates an expectation, a fixed notion of how and who this person should be. Most of us have an idea of what we would like from love, and when a new romance doesn't match up with this idea we can hit unnecessary problems and even spoil a perfectly good relationship.

Marti, for instance, met the man of her dreams while on holiday. She told me they'd 'fallen crazy in love'. They talked every day online and soon he flew over from America, bringing with him an engagement ring. It seemed like a match made in heaven; they both worked hard, they both wanted children, they even laughed at the same things. But Marti felt there was something missing, and called me to say that she had doubts.

I was curious as to what the problem actually was. Did she not find him attractive? Was he difficult in some way? Marti assured me that all was fine in these respects.

'So what *is* the problem?' I asked her. She replied, 'He doesn't send me gifts and flowers every week.' To Marti, this was a sign that he didn't really love her. He called her every day to tell her how much he adored her, but her preconceived ideas nearly ruined a wonderful relationship.

Patrick had quite different expectations. He told me, 'I've met the girl of my dreams, but we never row. I am waiting for it to go wrong because all couples need to row.'

I asked him if there was anything particularly bothering him that he felt they needed to clear the air about. He replied, 'No, not at all.'

'So what would you argue about?'

Patrick looked stunned and said, 'Well, nothing'. But, he explained, his parents would have feisty rows and that was what kept their relationship strong.

Once I'd explained that not all relationships are the same, and that some couples really don't have much to row about, the pair settled into a calm and happy relationship.

Signs That You Have Met Your Perfect Partner

Here are a few signs to look out for if you think you have found your partner in life:

- When you first meet, you feel as if you recognise each other, even though you have never met before.
- You immediately act as if you are old friends and talk for hours.
- You have tastes in common; maybe you both love reading an obscure author or are hooked on a certain TV programme.
- Other people treat you as a couple as soon as you meet.

THREE STEPS TOWARDS FINDING
YOUR PERFECT PARTNER

To meet your perfect partner you need to start by taking a threefold approach; follow my step-by-step guide below to draw your ideal partner to you.

- Step One: use the Three Passageways exercise (see pp. 14–17) to clear any residue from the past.

- Step Two: let go of all your expectations and preconceived ideas. Many people tell themselves they have a 'type' – they are drawn to tall blondes, shy intellectuals or muscular men, for example. But by clinging to preconceptions we are liable to repeat unhelpful patterns. I have noticed that often when people finally meet their ideal partner they are the opposite of their usual 'type'. In fact, your ideal could easily be the last sort of person you would imagine. So let your mind be open and free of any fixed ideas. The Universe may just bring you a wonderful surprise.

- Step Three: to create the right vibration for meeting your ideal partner you need to bring your future love into the present time – the now – as if it is already happening. Once you know how it feels to be with your perfect partner your energy will rise to the correct frequency for it to happen. A good way to reinforce this is through the Snuggle-Down exercise opposite.

EXERCISE: SNUGGLE DOWN

This is a great exercise to do on a Sunday morning, or any day when you do not have to rush off to work.

Begin by opening yourself up, following the instructions on p. xxix. Then, relax deeply and imagine you have had the most refreshing sleep ever, just enjoy snuggling down under the covers feeling warm and cosy.

Imagine you have just woken up and your perfect partner is by your side. Just allow your mind to flow and get a sense of what it feels like to have your ideal partner snuggled up next to you. Get a real sense of how it feels.

What is your partner like? Don't impose your own ideas, but allow images and feelings to come to you. Are they big or small? Soft and cuddly? Smooth and firm? Be aware of how you feel: safe? Happy? Content? Amorous? Notice the feeling of closeness and connection.

Turn and face your partner. What does he or she look like? You may catch a glimpse of them, but don't worry if you cannot actually see them or make out their features: just get a sense of what they are like. What do your senses tell you?

Now become aware of your surroundings. Are you living in the same place? Where are you and your perfect partner living?

Next, imagine you are going about your day together. What are you going to do? Perhaps make breakfast together? Chat over coffee? Go out somewhere? Focus on where you will go and what you will do. Take time to focus on your perfect day with your perfect partner.

Now take yourself to the evening. Will you eat out or at home? What will you eat? How will you spend your evening – socialising, watching a movie or just chatting?

Get as many details as possible about your perfect day with your perfect partner. Make sure you really sense what it feels like, as if it were actually happening. This will create the right vibration to bring it about.

Now focus on your current time, snuggling down in your warm and cosy space.

Remember to end by closing yourself down (see pp. xxix–xxx). Afterwards, it would be good to write or record your experience of this exercise as a story to reinforce the vibration.

HAVING IT ALL

There is a lot of discussion these days as to whether women can 'have it all', and in reality it is not always easy to find the right balance. Our predecessors maintained set roles for men and women, and that conditioning can very easily filter down to us, often unconsciously. Even though today's aspirations and opportunities far exceed former expectations, women can still be held back by out-of-date beliefs unless these are identified and cleared.

Nadine's Story

Nadine bounced into my office, tall, slim and beautiful: with a string of successful television shows under her belt, you would think she had the world at her feet. Yet she told me, 'I really worry that I will never meet the right partner and have children. I am thirty-five now and feel that time is running out.'

Nadine went on to explain that her last relationship had

ended badly. On top of this she had some career decisions to make; she had received some interesting offers of work from America that could take her into the big time – but would this get in the way of her meeting Mr Right and having a family? In her own words: 'I could make a huge mistake. I so want to take my career further, but I don't want to sacrifice the chance of love for my career. I really need to know which way to go.'

It was clear that Nadine believed she could have either career or love, but not both. I suggested that she may have something to clear from her past, and took her through the Three Passageways exercise (see pp. 14–17) to discover what it was.

Nadine was drawn to the childhood passageway. As she entered it she became aware of her mother's negative attitude to 'career women'. She could hear her bitter voice saying, 'Men don't like career women. You can't have both. If you have a career no one will want you.'

I encouraged Nadine to find and cut a number of cords from her mother (see pp. 26–7), which she did easily; after this she was ready to focus on a better future.

We began by looking at her life in five years' time, assuming she stayed on her current path. This was the future she would have if she carried on with her current mindset and continued progressing at her current rate. Immediately, she smiled and said, 'I have children, I am so happy!' She described her house as cosy, but modest. However, there was a tinge of disappointment in her voice, so I asked her how she was feeling.

'I am so happy to have children and I am married to a sweet man, but I feel I could have achieved a lot more. And although he is sweet, I am not madly in love with him and I wish I'd done more with my career.'

I often ask my clients at this point to take a look at their life if they'd opted for other possibilities. In her second look at the future, Nadine saw herself in America. As she viewed this new option she looked surprised. 'I am in New York; I didn't expect that! I assumed I would be in LA.'

'Are you living there?' I asked her.

Her face lit up. 'Wow, it's a rather plush apartment, really quite something.'

'And who is in your life?'

'It's a different man, he is really high-powered. It is great to be around someone who is so successful, because life is exciting but ...' her voice trailed off. 'I don't feel happy. Why am I not happy?'

I told her to take her time to see what the problem was.

She said, 'I don't know who he is, but I have the impression he is quite a cold character, and he doesn't want children.'

'How is your career?' I asked.

'Very good. I've made a lot of money and have done very well in both films and television, but I feel quite empty inside. I really don't like this future at all.'

I brought Nadine back to the neutral place and told her, 'Now we are going to look at your best possible future. The one where you make the right decision and do what is right for you.'

Before I could finish speaking, Nadine said, 'I am in LA. I feel so happy. It's a gorgeous house, really lovely with a big pool and lots of lawns. I love this place – oh, and there are children, two little kiddies! They are so sweet.'

'Who are you married to?' I asked her.

'I am not too sure, I don't know him. He is clever and successful, but also very sweet-natured. He has strong family values, which I love.'

'And how is your career going?'

'Oh, brilliant! I am writing a lot and have my own television show. Things couldn't be better. I feel quite emotional looking at this. The main thing is I have love and children and a career.'

Afterwards, we discussed how Nadine's upbringing may have affected her decisions. As well as her mother, all the other women in her family had been home-makers and, although it was never directly said, she knew they disapproved of her work.

'I am so happy now that I know I can have both a family and career, and maybe my younger nieces will see that they can have the life they want too.'

Love creates an energy far greater than that of the people involved. The love energy flows outwards; it ripples out into the world and raises the vibration of the planet and its people. Just know the one thing the world needs right now is love. As you create love in your life that love will ripple outwards, creating a wonderful vibration all around you.

A MESSAGE FROM MY FUTURE SELF

CHAPTER 5

YOUR IDEAL WORKING LIFE

I magine being in your ideal line of work. You'd wake up in the morning excited about what the day would bring. You would use your abilities to the full and be respected for your achievements. You would enjoy the company of like-minded people. In this chapter I will be showing you how to make the most of your talents and move with the times.

We live in a period of great uncertainty. We've had a major world recession, mass unemployment and countries on the verge of bankruptcy, while widespread demonstrations have led to changes of government. Far from being in their ideal job, many people find it difficult to get any work at all, or fear for their job security, as businesses and organisations cut down their staff. The world of work is constantly changing and we need to change with it if we are to survive.

Only a generation or two ago a man could expect to stay in the same job for most of his life, often working for just one company. My granddad was an electrician and worked for the Electricity Board his whole life. Things have changed a great deal since then, and over the years I have seen many occupations simply disappear. For instance, I never dreamt there would come a time when milk wasn't delivered to our doorstep, but these days I rarely see a milkman; and I never imagined that you would be able to serve yourself at a petrol station, let alone buy petrol at the supermarket.

In more recent times, many professional people like architects and solicitors have come to see me because they have been made redundant and have no idea what to do next; when they started their careers, they thought they were secure for life. I have seen many businesses thrive and then fade away. Products go in and out of fashion; people lose interest. When I meet successful business people they invariably mention a business they once ran which was quite different from the one they are in now; people who know about business know the right moment to move on.

MOVING WITH THE TIMES

Today we need to be constantly re-evaluating, re-inventing and anticipating the future. The truth is you need to be more aware than ever of where you are heading. If you do not grow, you will slip behind. Of course, there are still people today who are in family businesses that have survived for many generations, but when I look deeper I find they have adapted and evolved with the times.

For example, a number of British retailers have gone into liquidation through not having had the foresight to build an online presence; successful retailers, on the other hand, are aware that shopping habits have changed, and that many people no longer go out for their weekly shop now that they can have it delivered. This is the kind of change that companies need to be aware of if they are to survive.

In my own case, work in the spiritual field has also undergone many changes in recent years. I started out like my grandmother doing readings at my kitchen table, but today I do them by email and conduct many sessions via Skype. I teach my global audience via webinars and can send out my newsletter to thousands of people at the press of a button.

Over the last ten years, I have worked with a wide variety of companies and individuals using FLP to help them find the best way forward. I have noticed that business people who have anticipated the future and embraced new developments are successful, regardless of the size or type of their business, from local restaurants and plumbers to large corporations. Anticipating the future makes all the difference between success and failure, and companies today cannot afford to get it wrong.

Whatever field you are in, it is likely to be changing, and to succeed you need to change with it. The key is knowing how and what to change. This is where FLP can be so useful, as Leon's story shows. In his case, using the Buggy exercise helped him to see exactly what he needed to do.

Leon's Story

Leon came to see me having been recommended by an associate who had turned his business around with my help. I could see that he was almost paralysed by the fear of making the wrong decision.

Leon had a business with two friends supplying engineers to companies. It had been very successful until the recession;

then, almost overnight, demand started drying up and several of the companies they supplied went out of business. They had now used up their overdraft and were finding it hard to pay themselves. Even so, Leon was afraid to let go in case things suddenly picked up again. He told me:

'The last few years have been a roller-coaster – my head is completely scrambled! I need to be able to anticipate the market. I need to know what will happen next. One minute things look as if they are picking up, the next it all looks set to crumble. I used to be confident and decisive, but business is so uncertain these days. I really need to know if things will pick up or whether we need to cut back or even give up.'

Leon spent some time telling me how, with hindsight, he wished he'd made changes earlier – a sure sign he needed to look back at his earlier options. The Buggy was the ideal exercise for him (see pp. 55–7). He needed to look at his earlier options in order to get a hook on where to head next.

We started by using the Buggy to look five years into the future and get an idea of how things would turn out with his present mindset. He told me, 'We are still struggling along, only now we are even more in debt. We are in a lot more trouble now.'

'What do you wish you'd done differently?' I asked.

'I wish we'd downsized a lot sooner. We are now in a position I don't think we can get out of.'

'Use the Buggy to go back to two years before the present time and see what you could have done differently,' I told him.

Leon sighed as he said, 'Two years ago we should have moved to less expensive offices and cut back on staff. We were worried our customers would lose faith in us, but that isn't the case – they are doing the same themselves. But it would still have been a bit late.'

'Okay, just allow the Buggy to take you back to the point when you could have made better moves.'

'Ah, I have gone back to four years ago. This is a lot better. We could have anticipated the market, got smaller offices and made some of our staff redundant. But we could have also made some clever changes by creating a bank of freelancers and experts we could call on.'

'How would things be now if you'd followed that line?'

As he envisioned this alternative present Leon replied: 'Calm, totally calm; I feel far more in control. The downsizing means we are ticking over, but we would no longer be under pressure and paying out lots of wages for people we don't need. And because I am not so tied up here I have looked for business elsewhere, and have had an offer to work overseas. My partners can hold the fort while I go off and bring in some money.'

'Now use the Buggy to look ahead five years from your present time if you'd followed that pathway.'

Looking at this future, Leon exclaimed, 'Wow, we are back on track! I pulled in some big contracts while I was overseas. We are moving upwards again. Hey – we are even taking back some of our old staff. I love this Buggy! In business we need to be constantly weighing things up and this is the best way. I will go on using it.'

'So,' I commented, 'now you have had insights from both the past and the future. Come back to the present time and see how they affect your decisions right now.'

'It's funny, but I know exactly what to do. I will get smaller and cheaper offices. There are several staff members I can easily lose – they don't seem too keen on work anyway! And I will start to look overseas for contracts. After all, some countries have plenty of engineering work going on.'

Leon popped back to see me several times to fine-tune his decision with my guidance. He wanted to make sure he never got stuck again.

WHEN CHANGE IS FORCED ON YOU

While some people can adapt their work or their business to the times, others may find that changes in the current state of employment push them on to a whole new career path. Many people who have been made redundant set up their own businesses, doing well as freelancers and often discovering talents they haven't used before. If this is the case for you, you can use exercises like the Buggy to look at alternative options before putting your redundancy package into something new.

Among my clients I have seen one lady start a cake-making business; she now has a market stall and supplies several cafés. Another client, a former senior executive, took a hairdressing course and set up a mobile barber business; now his new venture is booming and he is offering a service to many people who find it hard to get out and about.

Some problems, however, arise as you get older or suffer from health problems, as happened with Clive. Though he loved his work, he couldn't carry on with it, and came to see me feeling quite distraught.

Clive's Story

Clive was an exceptional builder; he had a big client base and had built up a lot of goodwill. He had trained as a plumber on leaving school, and added to his skills along the way. But the years of hard work had taken their toll; now he suffered constant pain in his back and knees. His doctor told him that if he continued working as a builder he would end up doing irreparable damage to his health. But if he gave up, how would he survive financially?

I took Clive forward to view his options in five years' time. As he viewed the first option, he sounded crestfallen. He had continued working, and was in severe pain. He told me, 'I've had to sell my house, this is terrible.'

Viewing the second option he said, 'This looks a little better. I stopped work sooner, and we moved to a smaller house. But I still left it too late and it is too painful to work.'

'So how are you living?'

'I have drawn my pension early and used it to reduce my mortgage.' He looked sad. 'This is a pretty austere way of life and I don't feel I am providing properly for my family.'

Clive was nervous about looking at his third option, even though it would show him his best possible future. Sometimes when people are feeling down it is difficult for them to think beyond their current limitations. So instead I took him forward to his next lifetime, where he could get advice from his highly evolved Future Self.

His Future Self told him, 'With all these years of experience and all the expertise you have gained, can you not think of a way to put these to good use?'

Clive shrugged and said, 'I feel a little daft talking to myself here. Hold on – he wants to show me something!'

Clive saw an image of himself standing up in front of a group of around twenty young people. 'This doesn't make any sense,' he said.

I told him to look back to the time when his life started to go in a new direction. He said, 'Hm, it seems to be quite soon. Oh – I have a couple of apprentices, I am training them up. They are really keen.' Then he added, 'One of them is my nephew Sean; my brother said he was good with his hands.'

Clive was soon flooded with images of the future. He would be running the business, leaving the hard physical work to the young team he had trained. 'It's great to be able to give these lads the opportunity to learn a trade,' he said.

I asked him how his back was faring in these images. 'It seems much better,' he said. 'Having less stress seems to make a difference. But I still can't understand why I saw myself standing up in front of a group of youngsters.'

After this session, Clive kept in touch and it was interesting to see how things progressed. Two years later he was running his business and overseeing his young team; in addition, he was teaching plumbing part-time at his local college. He said, 'If you'd told me I'd end up teaching, I would never have believed it! But here I am, loving every day – and pain-free, to boot.'

Five years later Clive had sold his business for a sizable sum and had paid off his mortgage. He was still teaching part-time at the local college, though, which he thoroughly enjoyed. He commented, 'The last thing I expected was to be teaching. I had to see it for myself, because if anyone else had told me what I'd be doing I'd have thought they were potty!'

CREATING CORDS IN BUSINESS

Every time you do business with someone you create a cord. Often when people work closely together a great many cords are formed and they become bonded. The people who run successful companies have realised this and use it to their advantage. In the past, as long as people did their job well, the managers were satisfied. But then they began to notice the value of people working as a team; when employees 'connected' with each other, their motivation was stronger, their work improved and they had greater job satisfaction.

To strengthen these bonds, many companies have started to put on social events, such as team-building weekends, but as a result, the company tends to become the employee's whole life. Some of my clients have told me that they would really like to change their jobs, but fear that if they move elsewhere they will lose all their friends and social life.

So whereas previously a good boss would create that powerhouse effect themselves by reinforcing the admiration and loyalty of the workforce, these days bosses are so busy team-building and creating attachments between their staff that they rarely become revered themselves.

One person who does have this skill down to a fine art, however, is Richard Branson. If you meet any of his staff, from senior management to the tea-lady, they speak with great pride of working for him, even if they've never actually met him. Such admiration must energise him, which is why he is a fantastic leader. His staff all connect with a little bit of his greatness.

EXERCISE: BUILDING HELPFUL CORDS AT WORK

If you have worked with etheric energy cords as described in Chapter 1 (see pp. 19–30), your awareness of them will have grown so that you are ready to discover how to build them between yourself and your colleagues. Make sure you remember to open yourself (see p. xxix) before starting this exercise.

I am sure that, at times, when you have been dealing with people in a work or personal situation you have been aware of an energy between you, sometimes positive, sometimes less so. Often, we are too busy to stop and take notice, but most people will have had times when they have experienced this strongly. You may feel a tingle in your tummy or a pressure in your chest; you could have a desire to step back from them or you may be strongly drawn to them and the way they work.

As you work alongside your colleagues, spend a moment sensing their energy. You may be able to tell how they are feeling. Are they nervous, or confident?

Allow your aura to grow bigger and brighter. If you are working in a group, allow strands of your etheric energy to touch each of your colleagues positively. Focus on having positive feelings towards them and whatever you are working on. Allow your aura to flow around the group, as if pulling everyone together with positive energy.

End by closing yourself down, following the instructions on pp. xxix–xxx.

My clients who have practised this report that groups who are usually very difficult to work with have suddenly let go of their barriers, working as a team and helping each other. You can also use this exercise if you have a colleague who is particularly difficult to work with. Rather than feeling antagonistic, simply send them a stream of your etheric energy and notice how they open up to you.

Corporate Guidance

The corporate world has taken a big interest in Future Life Progression and I have been invited to work with a wide range of companies and their employees, from Hollywood film companies to accountancy firms, from large software corporations to training schools.

I recently visited a large company where I took some of the employees into future lifetimes. The aim was to look into the long-term future of the company and for the employees to gain insight from their future selves. Each employee saw what work they would be doing next time around and the skills they will have acquired. Often this gives them a clue as to what they need to develop in their present life.

Seeing our role in our next lifetime gives us an idea of the direction we need to develop and what our future strengths will be. Sheila, for example, was a PA and had always stayed in the background, but after seeing herself in a managerial role in her next lifetime, she took the plunge in her present life and went for a higher position with more responsibility. She now manages a team of ten people and they are thriving.

FINDING A DIRECTION

Quite a number of people these days have no real direction, whether at the start of their working life or, quite often, part of the way through. A businessman recently came to see me and said, 'This sounds silly, but I don't know who I am or what I am meant to be doing.' Nothing in his life felt right.

This can be the case too with celebrities or sportsmen when they have reached the peak of their careers: they have fulfilled their original burning ambition, and now they feel flat. There are also those people who have never found anything they particularly want to do.

The shortage of available jobs makes people feel additionally unmotivated, but motivation is what you need when you're looking for work. The Past, Present and Future Lifetimes exercise below is perfect for those who have no idea what they want to do, and really need to see the bigger picture. It takes people out of themselves and provides them with an overview of their soul path. It gives them an inkling of what they are meant to be doing, which is often very different from what they may have imagined.

EXERCISE: PAST, PRESENT AND FUTURE LIFETIMES

Start, as usual, by opening yourself up (see p. xxix).

You find yourself sitting in a peaceful meadow. You can feel the warmth of the sun on your skin; you can hear a gentle breeze rustling through the leaves on a nearby tree. In front of you is a stream; you watch the flow of the cool, clean water. You take off your shoes and feel a tingle as you dip your toes into the stream. There is no one about as you enjoy this special place.

You look up at the sky: it is the most perfect blue, with an occasional small white cloud drifting by. You feel yourself relaxing and letting go, and as you let go of yourself you somehow feel lighter in yourself, lighter and unburdened.

As you sit and enjoy this feeling of lightness you notice you are gently floating upwards, and as you float upwards you feel yourself letting go even more. In fact, the higher you float the more relaxed you feel.

Now you find that you are looking down on yourself. Down below you can see yourself sitting in the meadow with your toes in the stream, looking very happy and peaceful.

As you look down, think about your life and focus on what you would like to gain from this meditation. Just know that by gaining insight into your past and future you will be able to find your true path in your current time.

You may become aware of patterns that have run through many lifetimes and may even continue way into the future to your next lifetime.

Still looking down, you notice that you are beginning to float backward, back through time. You are floating back through your younger years, back through your childhood and back to when you were a baby. Now you are floating back to the time before you were born, towards a past life, one that is important for you to connect with right now, which will give you the information that you need.

Now float above that lifetime, look downwards and float down into that past lifetime.

Get a sense of where you are and what you are doing. Do you have any skills? What is your role? Get a sense of what you do with your time that fulfils you.

Once you have gained the information you need, let yourself float back upwards until you are hovering over your past self. If there is something in that past life you need to let go of, then allow yourself to let it go. Float back to your present time, and look down on yourself sitting with your toes in the cool stream.

Now float forward and keep floating forward until you are above your next lifetime. Get a sense of where you are and what you are doing. What is your vocation? What is your greatest skill?

Speak to your Future Self and ask for guidance. Ask what you need to be doing right now to forward your career. What direction do you need to take?

When you are ready, float back above yourself in your current time. Be aware of any skills or abilities that connect your past and future lives. Take time to review what you have seen and how it can help you right now.

Once you have gained all the information that you can, gently float back down until you are feeling the cool tingle of the water in the stream. Be aware that somehow you are different, something has changed. Be aware that you can now walk your career path and truly make the most of your skills and find fulfilment in your work.

Remember to close yourself down at the end of the exercise (see pp. xxix–xxx).

Job Hunting in a Recession

In the last few years, as the recession has kicked in, I have had numerous new clients needing career guidance – people who have been in great demand in the past, but whose work has now dried up or who have been made redundant.

At first, they are optimistic; they rewrite their CVs, sign up with agencies and expect to get snapped up in no time, as would have happened previously. A few months later, they are still upbeat, but surprised to find they have not had an interview or even a reply in some cases. After two years, the

▶

once dynamic, successful person has no idea where to go next. They've tried everything they can think of; got in touch with every possible contact, joined networking clubs and taken up golf, all without success. In short, they have run out of ideas and resources. By the time they visit me they are often depressed, feeling they have no further options to try and no future.

I find the Past, Present and Future Lifetimes exercise really helpful for these clients because it lifts them out of their current dilemma and gives them an overview of their entire path, not just their current difficult situation. Often, they gain helpful insights and guidance from their Future Self which helps them to discover a new path – one they had not previously thought of. The best part is when I get the phone call telling me that things are now going great.

A lot of the people I come across in my work feel trapped or stuck – and once you are stuck in a rut it is difficult to imagine a way out because it limits your thinking and you cannot see beyond your present problems. Weighing up options is impossible when you don't feel you have any.

By rising above the situation and getting an overview of your past, present and future, you gain answers; you acquire a clearer picture and you can clearly see what you need to do and what you need to let go of, like my clients Linda and John.

Linda's Story

Linda felt unfulfilled in her work as a dental nurse. She was good at her job but was simply not happy. She told me, 'I can't bear to look in one more person's mouth!' Unfortunately, however, she had no idea what else she wanted to do and, with bills to pay, she felt trapped.

We began by looking at Linda's past life. As her previous life came into view she said, 'Oh I am massaging someone's head, how odd.'

Linda saw herself in Sri Lanka. She described her delicate features, her softly tanned skin and her colourful sari. She explained, 'I am using my thumbs to put pressure on certain points of my patient's skull. He has been suffering with terrible headaches, but when I work on him the pain disappears and he looks so peaceful now.'

I asked her, 'So what is the main message from your past life?'

Linda smiled and said, 'Well, at least I am working on the right part of the body with my day job, but really I am a healer. I already know I have a natural ability and now is the time to use it. I have been drawn to working with people and that part of the body for a reason.'

Next, I took Linda forward to see her future lifetime. Once again she described working on patients' heads, but this time there was a laser-like energy coming from her hands, a stream of multicoloured lights that targeted certain points on the head.

Linda spoke excitedly. 'There is this powerful energy pouring from me. It is so bright I am screwing up my eyes, but this energy cures pain and many health problems in seconds.' She then said something very interesting: 'The odd thing is I am sure it is the same patient that I worked on in my past life.'

Usually when I am conducting a past or future life session I catch glimpses of what is happening. I told her, 'I didn't want to lead you, but I had the same feeling. In fact, I was sure you also become lovers.' As we chatted afterwards, we both had a strong feeling that 'the patient' would reappear at some point in her current life.

Shortly afterwards, Linda took an Indian head massage course. Afterwards, she called me to say, 'I recognise the tutor. I am sure it's *him*, and he has hinted we should get together outside the class.'

Often, when we find our true path, other areas of our life begin to open up to new possibilities as well.

John's Story

At forty-seven, John still had no clear direction in life. He told me, 'I am a dabbler. I dabble in this and I dabble in that, but I never really find my true path. I envy people who know exactly what they want to do.'

Over the years John had taken courses in art and creative writing, had joined a meditation group and did yoga. He'd been on numerous workshops, but as soon as he'd finished one, he was off to try something new. He was a smart fellow and I had the feeling that if I took him forward in his current time we would just find more of the same.

Indecisiveness is common these days as people have far more choice than in the past. Think back to your grandparents and how limited their opportunities were; for many the options were working in a local factory, farm, mine or dockyard. Today it could be said that we have too much choice: with so many possibilities we can lose sight of what might be our true vocation.

I decided that John needed an overview of his past and future lifetimes. There is often a theme running through our lifetimes which can be a good indication of our talents and what we are meant to be doing.

First, I took John to view a past life. He soon became aware of who and what he was.

'I am an American Indian brave, I teach the younger braves. I show them how to make arrows and how to fish. I teach them hunting and combat, and how to mount a moving horse. I give them confidence. I bring out their abilities.'

'How do you do that?'

'I can see inside them and know what skills are in their hearts. This is my life and what I was born to do.'

'How can you teach so many different skills?'

'Because I have learnt them all myself. It is the only way.'

In his past life John had certainly found his true vocation and made the most of acquiring lots of skills. Unlike the John of today he didn't beat himself up, but instead passed those skills on to others. I was curious as to what he would be doing in his next lifetime, which is where I took him next.

Even by our very next lifetime, our future selves often seem to be far more together, doing what they love and engaging in activities that resonate with their personal gifts and beliefs. Often, visiting our future lives can show us what we need to be working towards right now.

John is a big, burly man so we were both surprised when

he entered his next lifetime and announced: 'I am a woman. I am tall, very tall, but very feminine.'

'What is your role? What do you do?'

'I take people, young people who are lost and I help them. I teach them to look within themselves and find their true essence. I teach them many things, so they get a sense of what they are naturally good at and enjoy. These are young people who have never had the chance to look within and find out who they truly are.'

I instructed John to speak to his Future Self and ask for guidance. After a few minutes' silence he said, 'She seems surprised that I am not already doing this work. I have the range of knowledge, so why am I not passing this on to those who need it? I've never thought of it that way before.'

After the session John said, 'You know I've been beating myself up, when I should have realised I was amassing all this knowledge and skill for a purpose. A friend of mine runs a group for disadvantaged children – I shall call in there on my way home. I think I might just be able to help the kids discover some talents they didn't know they had.'

The last I heard, John was running his own group as well as working with his friend. He'd finally found his true vocation.

WHAT'S HOLDING YOU BACK?

All too often, people's lives are less than fulfilled because they hesitate to make the most of their opportunities. Too late, they look back and wished they had done more, or been braver.

Many years ago I lived near an elderly man. Each day as I passed his little house we would exchange a few words. Some days he would mention the weather, or who had visited him, but often he would tell me his regrets. His favourite saying was, 'I wish I'd ...' He would tell me how he wished he'd bought his council house when it was on offer for a pittance. Or how he wished he had travelled the world, or taken up art, or, when he had the opportunity, bought shares in the Channel Tunnel for a penny each.

One day I asked him why he had held back on so many things that he now wished he had done. He said, 'My first thought would be to do it – then I would think again, and think of all manner of reasons not to do it.'

The last time I saw him he told me, 'I have hesitated my entire life and lost so many opportunities that are now gone for ever.' He died a short time later.

The message here, loud and clear, is: hesitation alone can hold you back your entire life.

The following exercise will enable you to free yourself from anything that may be holding you back.

EXERCISE: BE ALL YOU CAN BE

First, open yourself up, following the instructions on p. xxix.

Imagine you are standing in the middle of a long and winding road. As you stand there, take some time to think about where you are right now: focus on your career and what you have and haven't achieved. Are you where you want to be? Have you progressed as much as you wanted? Or did you think you'd be further down the road by now? Take a few moments to focus on your current situation. Is there any frustration? Is there something you wished had happened but hasn't? Or have you pulled off something marvellous? Maybe got the job or promotion you wanted? Or succeeded in getting a big business deal? Take time to make an honest appraisal of where you are right now.

As you focus you will be aware of times when you have held yourself back. Maybe you didn't believe in yourself or had doubts for other reasons. Even a slight hesitation can lose you the opportunity you were hoping for. Focus on any lost chances and the breaks you should have got but didn't.

As you look honestly at your successes and failures you will bring up the emotions that you need to clear. Soon you will be rid of them, but for now notice what emotions come to the surface. Notice if there are any physical sensations in your body – maybe tension in your forehead or a nauseous feeling in your stomach. If you don't feel anything physically, just be aware of the area of the body the emotion comes from and know that this is where the etheric energy cords from the past are attached to you (see pp. 19–30).

Once you are aware of the location of the cords, float upwards and look down on yourself. Observe the cords and know that they keep you attached to the negative energy that holds you back from being all you can be. Be aware of what emotion is within the cords. Think of one word to describe that emotion. Perhaps fear? Greed? Anger? Doubt? Suspicion? Uncertainty? Allow the word describing your emotion to come to you. If there is more than one word you can carry out the cutting process more than once, but for now focus on the one emotion you most need to clear.

As you look down on yourself and observe the cords, focus on the word you have chosen and be aware of the origins of these cords. Know that these cords are full of emotion, emotion that blocks you from using your skills and abilities and creating the success you want. Are they from your childhood, ancestry or from a past life? Allow the answers to come to you. You can even imagine you are back in the cave looking at the Three Passageways to find the source of the problem.

Identify the cord or cords you need to release. Now take your laser scissors (see p. 27) and cut through the cords. Actually feel the cords recoil away from you as you slice through them.

Once you have cut through the cords, take a moment to notice how you feel now that you have released the negative emotions.

Afterwards, notice how you have a new spark in you. Do you feel bolder, clearer and ready to be all you can be?

End, as usual, by closing yourself down (see pp. xxix–xxx).

Martin's Story

Martin was a successful comedian – successful in the sense that he was always working and was a popular character on the comedy circuits. But somehow that big break remained elusive.

I've known Martin for a good few years, and have been to a number of his shows, but as he arrived at my office one day, his usual bubbly demeanour was noticeably missing. He slumped down in the comfy chair and said: 'I feel lost.'

Five years earlier, Martin had had an FLP session. At that time he was a rookie comedian trying to build his presence on the circuit. In that session he saw himself in a plush apartment and living with a girlfriend he described as 'lovely'.

Within two and a half years everything he had seen had

happened. Now he told me, 'I don't want to sound ungrateful because things have gone very well for me, but for the last two years I have been stuck. I know I am capable of so much more.'

My instincts told me that Martin had been holding himself back; it was almost as if he could only let himself have so much and no more. I decided to use the Buggy exercise with him (see pp. 55–7). This is ideal for taking people beyond any current limitations in their mindset to weigh up options and to fine-tune what they are doing.

Martin moved forward five years. He said, 'Well, I have done a bit better, but not much, It's all rather flat, really.'

I instructed him to come back to his present time and be aware of another pathway, one that looked very solid and straight. Martin rolled forward in the Buggy to a stronger future. He told me: 'I am doing really well, but this does not seem like me at all. I am wearing a flashy suit, smoking a big cigar and barking orders at people. I would never do that! What's going on?'

I asked Martin to take his time and focus on what was behind this.

He said, 'Ah, I get it! This is a new character, it's a sitcom – I have written it and star in it.'

'So how did all this start for you? Focus on when it began. Use the Buggy.'

Martin rolled back to his teenage years and said, 'Ah, I remember now. One of my first routines was to play an arrogant twerp. The audience loved it, but I worried people would think I was really like that and I let it fade. Now I can see that would work as a character; that would work, making fun of arrogant people's behaviour.'

I asked Martin to imagine that he'd developed that character and built on it, and to fully feel what that was like. I wanted him to build a new past that incorporated that character.

Martin said, 'Yes, I get it. I feel several other characters have come along as well.'

'So what happened in the timeline when the successful TV show was created? What did you do to make it happen?'

Martin replied, 'I kept doing my stage show, but incorporated the new character. He quickly became quite well known; we call him the arrogant buffoon. Then a producer asked me if I was interested in building a sit-com around him. Of course, I jumped at the chance.'

Now we needed to strengthen this timeline. I told Martin, 'Okay, great, now come back to your present time and really feel that all this has happened. You are now ready to integrate this into your current time.'

Then I took Martin forward five years to see where he would be.

'Oh, I can see a box set of DVDs with my picture on them. Wow, this is so cool! And there are several books. I now know that a number of characters I have rejected in the past have a lot of potential. I have been overly self-critical and worried about what people would think of me instead of just getting on and developing some great material.'

I could see a real shift in Martin's energy. He looked somehow more at peace with himself and also more self-assured. He was now ready for the big time.

The last I heard, Martin was in talks with several producers about a number of TV ideas. I can't wait to see him on television!

———————————

CHILDREN ARE THE FUTURE

One of the most fulfilling areas of work is helping young people to find their true vocation; while still in their teenage years they are expected to know what they want to do for the rest of their lives and have to make all-important choices with no experience of the world of work. They have to decide whether to go straight out to work or to apply to university or some other form of further education; if they opt for further study, they will need to be sure that they choose the best subject for them. They can easily be attracted to what they believe will earn them a lot of money or what is currently fashionable, rather than using their natural talents or picking a career that would give them genuine fulfilment.

I have worked with a great many teenagers to help them find their true path and have trained several schoolteachers who are aware of just how important it is for young people to make the right decisions at this crucial time of their lives.

If you have a teenager in your life who needs guidance, showing them their future career possibilities through FLP could be the best gift you could give them. Instead of being influenced by their peers or current fashions or, indeed, what their family are pushing them to do, you can guide them straight to what is ideal for them. Imagine not only helping them to make good choices, but also giving them the confidence to succeed in the line of work that they will enjoy the most and that best fits their skills.

Sam is a case in point. I first met him when he came to London from South America as a student to stay with a cousin. His aunt took me to one side and said, 'He'd love a session with you. He is in real turmoil as to which way he should go.'

That was some time ago, and over the years I have watched Sam's life unfold as he has transformed himself from a confused, awkward young teenager to a strong and successful man. His path was not an easy one, though.

Sam's Story

The men in Sam's family had worked in the diamond mines for generations, but what Sam really loved was numbers. He was not a physical person, and he wanted to be an accountant. At school he gained top marks in mathematics and his parents glowed with pride at his high grades.

At first they boasted about his gifts to the neighbours and extended family, but when Sam announced that he wanted to travel daily to another school to get some qualifications they were taken aback. They were still encouraging, but let it be known that they expected him to 'get a proper job' – by which they meant work in the diamond mines.

The new school was an hour's train ride away and to pay his fare Sam worked in his spare time for a local farmer. At the new school, he was encouraged by one particular teacher who believed he was bordering on being a mathematical genius and should go to university. He spoke about it to Sam's father, and was horrified when Sam's father said he expected Sam to go down the mines to bring some cash to the family.

This was Sam's problem when he came to see me. I decided to take him forward in time, so that he could weigh up his various futures. Sam felt there were just two options for him:

to do exactly what his family wanted or to follow his heart and study accountancy.

I first took him ahead ten years, to get a good idea of the total outcome of his decisions. As he looked at the first option of doing what his family wanted, his whole body slumped and he said, 'This is awful. I simply do not fit in here; my life is miserable.' He then added, 'I am not sure why, but the whole town is miserable. There is a general feeling of depression here.'

I quickly took Sam to his second option of further education. Instantly, he looked brighter. He said, 'I have qualified, and my life is wonderful! I am even married to a wonderful girl.'

I asked him, 'So how did you make it happen?'

'This must be fantasy because I am seeing myself studying at the top university. I could never afford to go there. I really don't know how it happened, but this is so real I must have faith that somehow I will get there.'

After the session he was even more determined to go to university, and on his return, with the help of his teacher, Sam won a scholarship. It was the opportunity of a lifetime and Sam couldn't wait to tell his family. He told me: 'I thought they would be happy about the scholarship. But you'd have thought by the looks on their faces I was about to go to prison.'

After this the family started to make little quips like, 'Sam must have been swapped at birth', or 'He is not one of us'. At first, their remarks seemed like light-hearted banter, but after a while they became more sarcastic and cutting, and Sam's family began to treat him like an outsider. He stuck to his guns, though, and went off to university. When he returned during the holidays, although his parents seemed pleased to see him, their manner was strangely distant, as though he had wronged them in some way.

While at university Sam met his future wife Cara, a kind and easy-going girl. He expected his relations to welcome her with open arms, but instead his female relations treated her with disdain. Gradually, Sam saw less and less of his family. He and Cara had two sons; when the boys were old enough to visit their grandparents and were also treated like outsiders he knew it was time to distance himself even further.

Sam called me from time to time, and he told me, 'I had to decide whether to confront them over their treatment of my wife and sons. I decided to walk away.'

I told him, 'Sometimes there is one person in the family who teaches the others. At some point this will turn around.'

Several years later Sam called me to say, 'The mine is closing and none of my family has any work, so they have no money. They have asked for my help. Also, one of my young nephews has my talent with figures, and has asked if he can work with me. Of course I said yes.'

Through Sam's determination to follow his path, he and his entire family eventually learnt a valuable lesson. Holding ourselves back in life does not serve us or anyone else.

Lars' Story

Lars had almost the opposite of Sam's problem; his family wanted the best for him. The problem was that he didn't know what he wanted, and needed help to discover what would be the best career for him. What looked interesting right now could turn out to be a poor career option in the future. He and his parents wanted to make sure he was on the right path.

Ever since he was a small boy Lars had been fascinated by chemistry. Instead of posters of football players or pop stars on his bedroom wall, he had the Periodic Table. But now in his teens, he was having second thoughts. He still loved chemistry, but had recently been drawn towards studying social science. Lars was confused and needed time to think, but time was the one thing he didn't have because soon he would need to choose what to do next.

His mother called me to ask for my help. She said, 'I have read about Future Life Progression and think it will help him to make the right choice.'

Lars was open to help and very easy to work with. As we chatted about his dilemma I had a niggling feeling that there was, in fact, a third option.

I took Lars three years ahead so that he could experience how he felt with each option. First we looked at him studying chemistry. He said, 'It's okay – just okay, nothing more.' His voice sounded flat. When I took him to the second option, social science, this too was, 'Okay, but nothing more'.

I said, 'Let's see if there is a third option. Maybe there is something you haven't thought of yet.' As soon as I spoke these words the energy changed; there was a sense of excitement about this option. Lars' expression told me he felt it too.

As he quickly reached the third option, he almost whispered, 'I am studying renewable energy. And I am loving it; it is really interesting.'

I wanted to know where this line of study would lead him, so I took him ten years into the future to check out all three options and discover how they would have panned out.

Firstly, we looked at his future in ten years if he'd studied chemistry. As before, his face fell as he said: 'Well, I am working and it is okay, but not very interesting.'

Next, we looked at the option of working in social science. I sensed he was not getting the opportunity to use his skills, especially his ideas and creativity. Lars had a really innovative streak and it would be a shame not to use it. That was what would give him fulfilment.

Then we looked at the third option and again he was working with renewable energy. His excitement bubbled over as he talked about working on exciting new projects with a brilliant team of experts and travelling to other countries to share their findings. As he spoke, he had an air of confidence; he sounded authoritative. I knew that in the future he would be a spokesperson for the industry, developing new ideas and inspiring others to do the same.

Lars had found his subject and could hardly wait to get studying.

At any one moment we all have choices, and the choices we make shape our futures. They could be anything from whether to have a day off and phone in sick to studying a new subject to strengthen our position; they could involve whether to ask for a raise or promotion or just sit tight. Or perhaps we need to decide whether to specialise in a certain field or to take a completely new direction. All of these choices have consequences, sometimes far-reaching, and if we get them right, we can fast-track to a brilliant future instead of wasting time heading in the wrong direction or even just being stuck, like Martin.

I want you to know that when you discover your true vocation you also discover your gift to the world and your own part in the universal plan.

Observe people who are successful and happy. They focus on what they are giving out, not on what they are receiving. They focus on their contribution. Notice now happy they are because their life has meaning and purpose.

Each and every person is here to contribute; both a beggar and a queen are humble servants of the world. It is easy to lose sight of this, but find your vocation and you will find your contribution and thus your own inner fulfilment. The biggest regret you will have is to let emotions, especially fear, stop you from being all you can be.

Fear generates a weak energy that creates doubt within you, and also doubt in others, and you will wonder why you are not getting the breaks. Fear will make you hesitate and make you self-conscious. It tells you that you will fail; it will make you worry and hesitate.

Fear will tell you that you need to know more and that you are not ready. Held back by fear, your journey will be slow and full of obstacles.

Rid yourself of the energy of fear, cut the cords, and you will fly.

A MESSAGE FROM MY FUTURE SELF

CHAPTER 6

CREATING WEALTH

Like many people today, you may have money problems, but you still have a choice of potential futures. This chapter will show you how to choose a future in which you are more prosperous. But first we need to discover if there is anything blocking your way.

Money is a form of energy. When your energy is vibrant, abundance naturally flows your way; but when it is low you can find yourself stuck in the poverty trap, trying to claw your way out and never quite making it.

Wealth is an area that particularly carries patterns from the past. Many people who are suffering from financial hardship today are carrying poverty patterns from past lives, childhood or ancestry. So the first thing to do is to use the Three Passageways exercise (see pp. 14–17) to find out where your problems started. In my own experience, ancestry has played a great part, and I find that is the case with many of my clients.

IF YOUR ANCESTORS WERE POOR

My own ancestors on both sides of the family suffered great poverty. My maternal grandfather went through extreme hardship in Ireland – hardship that had already been carried down through the generations. He used to tell me stories of how his mother suffered because the family never had enough to eat.

When he was just seventeen my grandfather came to England to work, and his fortunes began to change. However, even though he eventually made a comfortable living, he bore obvious emotional scars. The imprint of centuries of family poverty filled him with a fear that created many problems in his life; these, in turn, created problems in the lives of his children. Such patterns can pass down through generation after generation. Yet all it needs is for one person to break the pattern and create a more positive vibration that will then be passed down to their children.

My father's side of the family worked 'below stairs' in the stately homes of the gentry. My grandmother was a maid and my grandfather a Master of Ceremonies. My dad often told me how he used to watch his father announce 'the toffs' as they arrived at huge social events. Dad grew up with this total contrast: spending time in the grandest hotels in London and then going back to the tiny, shabby house in Islington which was home. At the age of eight he saw his father die of a stroke, and while his siblings were placed in an orphanage, he was the only one to remain with his mother.

In his latter years I used to take Dad for tea at the Ritz or for a stroll along Bond Street. He would beam with delight, and remark: 'Look how the other half live!' He was sure that the invisible divide was unbridgeable; he used to say, 'You must know your station in life.' He loved our outings, but felt more at home in the Portobello Road in Notting Hill, where I grew up. He worked hard and earned a very good wage, but he never lost his poverty consciousness.

Influenced by both my ancestry and my childhood, I myself struggled financially for most of my earlier life. Even when I made money something would happen to take it away; my car would break down and need expensive repairs, or I would become ill and be unable to work.

Over the years I read hundreds of books, had therapy and listened to CDs on prosperity, but still this pattern remained. Nothing changed until I recognised and cleared the poverty patterns I had inherited, and so created an abundant life for myself.

Laurelle's Story

Laurelle is a healer and Reiki Master. I read her story on her blog (Laurelle Shanti Gaia, www.reikiclasses.com) and liked it so much I asked if I could use it. It shows how she dealt with the patterns she inherited from her ancestors.

'I have become keenly aware of the energetic effect that my ancestors have on who I am, and also the energetic effect that I have on my children. I recognize now that I have been holding genetic coding [by which DNA stores genetic information] from my ancestors, which affects my cellular memory [inherited pattern], and in turn influences the patterns in my subtle energy system. Therefore, I make choices in my life based in part on the beliefs, experiences, feelings and thoughts of my ancestors.

'If we think of the challenges and triumphs of our ancestors we can often see how or where we are personally affected by them.

'Let me give you an example. I learnt that many of my issues involving self-worth, prosperity and work ethics go back through many generations. Although I feel that I have come a long way in healing them, I still see traces of these issues in my life daily. I am developing clarity on healing issues that some of my ancestors did not complete in their lifetime, and thus passed on to me genetically.

'Many of our parents and grandparents lived through the Depression in the 1930s, and I imagine some of you reading this did also. Living in that time created much fear for the ability to survive. It also brought up self-worth issues for many and created a workaholic consciousness in some. Many people felt powerless to change their circumstances.

'One day while I was sending healing energies to my ancestors I felt a particularly strong connection to my paternal grandmother. She lived the nightmare of the Depression when she and her family lost everything they owned except a piece of land in Illinois. For a period of time they lived in a small barn on their property, and they farmed the land to feed themselves and help their neighbors. The earth sustained them through this difficult time, and ultimately they were able to re-establish financial stability. However, this experience further instilled several beliefs in my grandmother, who already had lived through some very challenging times as a child.

'I felt her fear, sense of hopelessness, unworthiness, and I also felt the anchoring of the belief that life is hard, and that we must work very hard for everything we receive.'

Laurelle had clear images of her grandmother up before dawn gathering vegetables and eggs. She saw her rushing to get ready to go to work. She saw her sitting at a sewing machine in a factory.

She also saw the look on the faces of both her grandparents when they realised they'd lost their home. They appeared ashamed, sad and almost hopeless. She then had images of her grandmother in the barn, trying to make it comfortable as a home. She was aware that her grandmother was so tired she could not sleep.

'Although my life as a child was materially much easier than my grandmother's, and my parents did their best to provide for all of our needs, genetically the energetic essence of her fears and beliefs were passed on to me. In order to provide for our family, my parents "worked very hard" and sacrificed many of their personal emotional needs. Although my parents are both basically positive people, I still received messages from them or other family members such as: "Life isn't always fair"; "Only hard work and perseverance win out"; "If you are going to do something, do it right"; "Always put others' feelings before your own"; "In the end you can only count on yourself," and so on.'

Laurelle became aware that these patterns could carry on down to her own children and she was determined that this would not happen. She said, 'There are many "could haves". My children could have developed a fear of lack, or a sense that the "other shoe will drop" any minute. They could have developed workaholic habits or even miserly qualities.' Laurelle was determined that these patterns would stop right now.

As she sent healing energy to her ancestors she was aware

of a shift within them as if the past had somehow changed. She could also sense some shifts in her son, as if something had been released.

By sending healing energy to her ancestors Laurelle cleared her patterns right there and then, allowing herself and her family to prosper.

———————————

Laurelle's way of releasing her ancestral patterns was to send healing to her ancestors. This is something anyone can do: as I mentioned in Chapter 1 (see pp. 19–20), sending healing thoughts or prayer through our etheric cords, not only to those we care for in the present, but to people or situations from the past, can be very effective.

HELD BACK BY SHAME FROM THE PAST

At times, some of the people I work with have felt resentment towards their ancestors for actions that seem brutish or selfish by today's standards.

As my client Joanie put it, 'Knowing my great-grandfather gambled every last cent makes me so angry. I cannot find any justification for what he did. That money could have made my great-grandmother's last few years so much easier. Instead, she died in poverty.'

As we uncover the stories of our ancestors we may find that they did some bad or even terrible things. Rather than judging them, we need to simply clear the energy and release them. Everyone makes mistakes, everyone gets things wrong, and that is what makes us human. But by focusing on our ancestors' mistakes we reinforce the negative energy and attract more of the same. The important thing is not to carry that energy or emotion with us.

Girum's Story

Girum, in his late twenties, is an entrepreneur whose family is from the Far East. He had emailed me several times asking for an appointment, but would always cancel at the last minute with the excuse that he was too busy. Eventually, however, he made it to my office. He told me, 'I feel like a failure. I've started many businesses and they've all failed. I can't work any harder than I already do. I seem to start off well enough, but each time, just as I'm about to make some real money, it all goes wrong.'

This is a pattern I see often; people who want to be successful, but somehow never quite get there. Often they are clever, talented and hard-working, but success eludes them. This is a sure sign that there is a block from the past; all we need to do is find it and clear it.

Although Girum had been hesitant about having a session in the past, he was now open to any suggestions and keen to find the root cause.

I took Girum to the Three Passageways cave (see pp. 14–17), where he chose the ancestral passageway. He commented, 'I feel bad about this because I feel as if I am blaming my ancestors for my own shortcomings.'

I told him, 'This is not about blame; your ancestors did the best they could at the time. But we do need to clear any patterns that are blocking you. You have a family of your own now to take care of and this is more important.'

Girum agreed and made his way down the ancestral passageway. He said, 'I know my family has been very rich in the past. I have heard many stories, but it will be good for me to see for myself.'

Girum went back through many generations of his family and, oddly, the further back he went, the richer his family was. He said, 'It seems we have gone downhill with each generation.'

'Go back to the origin of the problem,' I told him.

'I am not sure how far back I have gone, but it is a long way. One of my ancestors is a very wealthy merchant, just like his father and his father before him. In fact, there is a long line of wealthy merchants who handed down their expertise and trained their children to take over from them. They built a very strong foundation for their business. The younger members would gradually take over and look after the elders. They lived a very good life.'

'So what went wrong?' I prompted him.

Girum flinched, 'I have this terrible feeling of shame. The ancestor I can see bought and sold inferior cloth. He shamed the whole family; people complained, and we lost our good name. He was a very greedy man and we have all paid the price ever since.'

'How could things have been different?'

Girum thought for a while, then replied, 'Well, I can see that his usual supplier had let him down and he had the chance to make some quick money. He could have been patient and waited for better material.'

I told Girum to visualise that happening and then to imagine walking a new path back through the generations, where his forefathers prospered and patience and honesty were rewarded.

Girum spent some time making his way back, as he watched each generation trade honestly and build on their forefathers' foundations. Eventually he said, 'To think so many generations have paid the price for that one mean act!'

'It is time for that to change. Let's see how you are doing in the future,' I suggested.

I took him through the Buggy exercise (see pp. 55–7), so that he could find his most abundant future. At the end, he told me: 'You know, I am now doing very well. My business has taken off, but I am no longer rushing. It seems I have the same lesson to learn as my wayward ancestor. We both need to take our time and do things properly. I can see that I have always been rushing around red-faced, but getting nowhere; now I think things through and only supply the very best to my customers – and it is working.'

I had a feeling there was more. 'Is there anything else you are aware of?' I asked.

'Yes. I have set up a charitable foundation to help poor children back in my own country. I feel the need to give back and make amends for my ancestor's mistakes. My life seems to have more meaning now. Before, all I wanted was the big house and car, but seeing the difference I can make to those children makes it all so much more worthwhile.'

Girum has gone from strength to strength; he is now active in his local community and is teaching his children how to build firm and honest foundations for their own future.

SENDING HELP TO YOUR ANCESTORS

I have worked with clients who, no matter how hard they work or how careful they are with money, always end up poor. In almost every case we have traced these issues back to an early ancestor and discovered that the poverty energy originating with that ancestor has come down to my client through a line of generation after generation, until the present time.

My Future Self explained to me that when we strengthen this ancestral line we automatically strengthen our own lives. The key is to go back to your earliest ancestors. By helping them you can clear the past energy of poverty and each subsequent generation becomes more prosperous until the prosperity reaches you. This exercise can create a wonderful and rapid change within you and any of your surviving parents and grandparents.

EXERCISE: HELPING YOUR ANCESTORS

Allow plenty of time, turn off your phone and find a comfortable place to relax. Open yourself up, following the instructions on p. xxix.

Now, in your mind imagine that you can see a long line of your ancestors stretching back through time, almost as if they are waiting in line. Those nearest to you, you will probably recognise as parents and grandparents. As you look further back you may recognise your great-grandparents from photographs. But as you look even further down the line there will be faces unknown to you. Notice how they are dressed and how they look.

Starting at your present time, walk back along the line as far back as you can, keep walking back until you reach a very early ancestor. By now they may be very primitive. Imagine doing something to make their life easier and more prosperous. You may give them a pot of gold or simply more food to eat, or show them an easier way to do things. Take time to guide them and show them how their life can be easier and more affluent.

Notice how this new affluence has a knock-on effect on each of your ancestors down the family line; one by one they become richer. If you notice any weak links along the way (just as Girum did), stop and deal with them. Help them to find a better way. Do whatever you need to, to make the line strong again.

Watch your ancestral line become wealthier with any lack fading away to be replaced by abundance. This can mean anything from having enough food to eat to ancestors who are already wealthy becoming far richer than before.

Be aware that as you have had help from your Future Self you are now doing the same. You are now a visitor from the future helping your ancestors.

Spend as long as you wish on this exercise, and go back as many times as you like to strengthen this line. When you finish the exercise, remember to close yourself down (see pp. xxix–xxx).

WHEN YOUR PARENTS' ISSUES
BECOME YOURS

The influences in our childhood, of course, play a part in all our attitudes to life. Many of today's baby-boomers had parents who struggled during the Second World War, when food was rationed and often the main breadwinner was away fighting. I find that many of this generation have a problem receiving wealth, often believing they don't deserve it.

In more recent times children have watched their families struggle during recessions, when a parent may have been made redundant or simply cannot make ends meet. Either way, the philosophy of our parents, and also our teachers, can have a powerful effect on our success and finances. This was the case with Emma, an old friend of mine.

Emma's Story

For as long as I can remember Emma has wanted to be rich and successful. Whenever we met up she would tell me about her latest venture. Emma has brilliant ideas; she also has the talent and the energy to succeed, but somehow she never made any real progress.

Over the years I watched Emma put vast amounts of energy into her work. At times, she would make a big splash, and then suddenly stop. At others, she would keep changing direction, jumping from one venture to another. Finally, her friends were getting fed up with her; she was becoming more erratic, often promising them the earth then letting them down once again.

I knew Emma had a good heart and desperately wanted to change the pattern. She was highly trained in a number of therapies, but always felt she needed to learn just one more – a pattern I often see with therapists. She also wanted to get involved with property, drawing on a small inheritance.

I'd offered to help on a number of occasions, but each time Emma assured me things were fine, she'd just had a few setbacks. Finally, one day she came to see me in desperation asking, 'What am I doing wrong? I am working so hard and I am good at what I do.'

Emma was actually sabotaging herself, confusing activity with achievement. Each time one of her many projects was taking off, she would drop it to try something else. I suggested we use the Three Passageways (see pp. 14–17); we needed to find the root cause of her behaviour. As we reached the mouth of the cave, she said, 'I don't want to look; this is not relevant to me. I do not have any blocks.'

I tapped into her and felt real fear. I tried coaxing her, but she was adamant that she didn't need any help. There was nothing more I could do.

It was three months before Emma called to tell me she was struggling more than ever and wanted my help. She was now using her inheritance to live on and it was dwindling fast.

Over coffee I explained how blocks tend to get worse over time and that I could see she was sliding backward at an alarming rate. Again Emma insisted she had nothing to clear; she just needed me to give her some positive energy. Luckily, I managed to persuade her 'to take a little look, just in case'.

Finally, she agreed. As she reached the mouth of the cave I could see her trembling; this lady had a deep-seated issue that was ruining her life. My clients usually view their past in a detached manner; I'd never seen any shaking or upset before.

I instructed her to allow the fear to flow away, and soon she relaxed and chose the childhood passageway. She said, 'I am aware of my family. They are saying, "Things are going too well; it's bound to go wrong." Now they are talking about my uncle who did well in business. They are saying he never mixes with anyone. They are calling him a mean old man.'

Emma was receiving floods of memories.

'Go back to the earliest incident that affects you right now. You don't need to experience them all,' I told her.

'I can see myself as a little child. I've been helping my neighbour with her garden and now she has given me an envelope with some money and called it my "pay packet". I am so proud and have rushed home to show my mother.'

Emma's pleasure turned to sadness as she said, 'My mother looks angry. She tells me to stop showing off because people will not like me. She says that I need to be careful or I will get mugged, flashing money around. It was only a few coins!'

I instructed Emma to imagine that the incident had been different, perhaps seeing her mother praising and congratulating her. 'See things as you wish they had been,' I told her.

Emma created images of a past in which her family had encouraged her and were proud of the successful uncle. Then she walked back through time, building more and more positive images. When she returned to the mouth of the cave she looked a lot more positive than when she began. She told me, 'I didn't realise it before, but my family always made me feel guilty if I had anything. Even my birthday presents were sneered at.'

When I last heard from her, Emma was making up for lost time and business was booming. She also decided to train with me in Future Life Progression, saying, 'If only I'd used this earlier! But at least now I can help others clear the way to success.'

———————————

Like Emma, many people sabotage themselves because they have been brought up to believe that being wealthy is a bad thing. While for some the idea of wealth brings feelings of happiness or security, for others it creates anxiety; they worry that it will turn people away from them or that they will lose their fortune. Before we go any further, I invite you to take a little time on the following exercise, and discover what abundance means to you.

EXERCISE: THE MEANING OF WEALTH

Find yourself a peaceful place to relax and let go of your everyday thoughts. Before you start, open yourself up, following the instructions on p. xxix.

Now, take time to stop and think about what abundance means to you. Usually our first thoughts are about big houses and flash cars, but as we allow our thoughts to settle something deeper often comes into play.

If your life were truly abundant, how would you feel?

Would you be happier, more secure, content, or perhaps worried or stressed?

Allow your thoughts and feelings to rise to the surface.

Now focus on the most positive thing wealth could bring you: perhaps more time with your loved ones, maybe a chance to help those less fortunate or your own personal secret hideaway. Would you move to a bigger home? Have more holidays?

How would it help you to contribute to your family, friends and the planet?

And how would you be in yourself – happier? More relaxed? Healthier? More secure?

Take time to notice how abundance would make you feel.

Allow your mind to flow freely and discover what abundance really means to you.

At the end of the exercise remember to close yourself down (see pp. xxix–xxx).

As always, note your thoughts down afterwards in your journal. If the idea of abundance makes you feel uncomfortable, you can use the Three Passageways (see pp. 14–17) to discover the origin of your discomfort or Cutting the Cords (see pp. 26–7) to release yourself from any unwanted beliefs that others have imposed on you.

PAST-LIFE POVERTY

Many of the most painful stories I have encountered have involved clients who have been servants or slaves in a past life. Often, we uncover stories of someone having been badly treated and physically abused. This can deeply affect them in their present life; they expect little for themselves and anticipate that bad things will happen if they ever ask for the tiniest bit more. There is usually a deeply held unconscious belief that they are not meant to be wealthy, or even comfortably off. When I have worked with these people, many of them talk themselves down, telling me they are not very clever or able.

Sara's Story

Sara was aware of issues that deeply affected her whole family. She'd worked relentlessly on herself – she'd read books, listened to CDs and seen counsellors – but just couldn't seem to find the crux of the problem. She had an inkling that if she could clear whatever it was from herself, then somehow her family would also be released. She was particularly worried about her brother Ryan, who was withdrawn and doing badly at school. In fact, he would do all he could to avoid going to school, and recently she'd seen marks on his arm, leading her to believe he'd been self-harming.

Surprisingly, when we did the Three Passageways exercise (see pp. 16–17) Sara chose the past-life passageway; I'd half expected her to be drawn to the ancestral one because she and her brother seemed to share some deep issue.

As Sara looked back through time she discovered that she had had the same people in her past-life family as she does today, though playing different roles, as is commonly the case – for example, your past-life mother may well be your sister, brother or daughter next time round. Often, we return with the same group of people – our soul group.

Sara became aware that her family was among the first Africans to arrive as slaves in the American Deep South. They were treated appallingly, constantly abused, beaten and insulted. Among other things, they were told they were worthless and stupid because they could not read and write. She visibly shuddered as she recounted the trauma. 'I have the same mother in that lifetime as now. I can see her looking down at the floor as her owner bullies and humiliates her. The worst thing is my father looks so ashamed that he cannot protect her.'

I asked her, 'Do you know your father from that lifetime in your current life?'

She sounded shocked as she said, 'Yes! He is my little brother who worries me so much.'

I suggested to Sara that we rewrite her past life and she readily agreed.

When I asked her how things could have been different, she replied, 'My parents were traumatised by the shock of finding themselves in such different surroundings and with such a different way of life. They believed what they were being told. They began to believe they were worthless.'

She added, 'The change I wish to put in here is for them to realise how wonderful they were.'

Sara then visualised herself working hard and gaining respect by teaching herself to read and write, and going on to teach her family and fellow slaves. She saw them prosper and educate themselves, then they, in turn, taught other slaves to read and write. She said, 'I can feel a real shift here, as if something has changed. I can see my father looking pleased with himself as he reads from a book.'

A few months later Sara told me that her brother had opened up and told her that he was really struggling to read and write. Sara arranged for him to be tested and they learnt that he was dyslexic. Now that Ryan had an explanation, and knew he was not stupid, he began coming out of his shell. His school gave him a specialist tutor and he was rapidly gaining confidence.

Sara told me, 'He has started to go out with friends and is dressing smartly. He is like a different lad. I suppose it could be a coincidence that he came to me straight after my session, but if it is, it's a very big one.'

———————————

I wonder how many dyslexics today had issues with reading and writing in their past lives.

CREATING ABUNDANCE

Many people dream of being wealthier, but it is often just a vague idea. Later you will be doing an exercise to enhance your wealth vibration, but first, the Castle of Abundance exercise will help you to define how your life would be if you were wealthier, and also how it would feel. Once you have the feeling of wealth you create an abundant energy that tells the universe: 'This is how my life should be.'

EXERCISE: THE CASTLE OF ABUNDANCE

Find yourself a comfy place to relax, unplug the phone and make sure you are not interrupted. Open yourself up, following the instructions on p. xxix.

Imagine you are walking along a country road on a spring day. Up ahead you can see in the distance a beautiful white castle. It is surrounded by a faint mist, giving the impression that it is floating. You know there is something very special about this castle.

You make your way along the country road towards the castle, and as you draw near you have a sense of anticipation. Soon you are standing in front of the moat around it. You look down at the deep moat and wonder how you will get across. At that moment the drawbridge lowers in front of you and you walk across it and go through the entrance.

You find yourself standing in a deserted courtyard. There is a great sense of peace as you look around and notice how immaculate everything is: the doors and windows are polished and the ground has been swept clean. But there is no sign of any people.

You stop for a moment to enjoy the tranquil surroundings and, as you do so, a small bird lands at your feet and starts pecking at the ground near by.

The bird begins to hop and chirp and you understand that it is trying to communicate with you. It hops across the courtyard towards a huge oak door. You realise that this is the main entrance to the castle and, as the little bird hops aside, you pull on the large handle and open the door.

As you walk inside you feel a shimmer of energy, a vibration that tells you that you have entered a very special place. You find yourself in a huge hallway; all around the walls are paintings of the previous owners.

Standing in the hallway you think about the ways in which you would like your life to be more abundant and what abundance means to you. Focus on the difference it would make to your life. Take some time to see your life full of abundance.

Now notice in front of you a large, sweeping staircase. Walk towards the staircase and make your way up the stairs, one step at a time. The staircase sweeps upwards to a floor high above you.

As you walk up the stairs you can feel something happening; you can sense a vibrating energy, and somehow you know this vibration is changing you. It is the vibration of abundance from your future self, from the wealthier future you.

As you walk up the stairs you can feel yourself changing. You have a new air about you, an abundant air. Somehow you are stronger. You attract abundance; wealthy people and situations are drawn to you.

Your mind is beginning to think in a more abundant way. As you continue walking up the stairs you can sense the changes: you walk taller, you expect abundance, you expect success.

Your attitude to money is now different. You know you can easily draw it to you. You have a knack of making money. You will look after your money and make wise decisions.

Soon you are reaching the top of the stairs and to the left you see a large drawing room; you walk inside and look around. The room is wonderful, with beautiful furniture and flooring, and it is perfect for you. Is the room modern or traditional? Look around and notice all the decorations – perhaps a crystal chandelier, luxuriously comfortable seating, maybe the softest of carpets. Is there a major feature in the room, like a huge mirror, or a magnificent painting, or a grand piano? Maybe you prefer a simpler style, but you see that everything around you is of the highest quality. Look around the room and, as you do so, feel at home, feel comfortable in these rich surroundings.

Take some time to absorb what it feels like to be truly wealthy. How do you spend your time? Are you generous, and if so who do you share your abundance with?

Spend time exploring your Castle of Abundance. You may walk around the grounds outside, or go to your main bedroom with its luxurious bed and furnishings. Maybe you have an office or sanctuary in the nearby tower. You can go anywhere you want to. Perhaps you meet friends, who are happy for your good fortune.

Spend as long as you wish in your castle, and know that you can come back here any time you want to. All you need to do is imagine walking across the drawbridge, back across the courtyard, into the main hallway and up the staircase, and you will feel your vibration becoming richer.

You can come here to think and make decisions, and to be inspired and connect with that powerful energy any time you wish.

When you have finished, walk back down the stairs, making sure you keep the abundant feeling with you, and walk across the drawbridge back to where you started, your vibration now richer and more abundant.

Now close yourself down (see pp. xxix–xxx).

I have used the Castle of Abundance with many clients and in workshops and seminars. After trying the exercise, my clients notice a big shift in how they feel and act in relation to money and wealth. Some become more aware of the value of investing or saving for the future, others become more businesslike. Still others have stopped procrastinating and have taken up a new study to further their careers or have asked for a promotion.

This is a good exercise to do regularly, perhaps once a week, to reinforce the abundant feeling and that of living a wealthy life.

PROPERTY MATTERS

At some point in most people's lives, property issues will arise, whether they are moving home, buying a house or flat, finding business premises or looking for a short-term rental. Making the wrong decisions can be catastrophic and not easily rectified. In fact, psychologists find that moving home is one of the highest causes of stress. (The mental-health charity MIND includes it in the five most stressful life events.)

By the time my clients get in touch about their property problems they are often at the end of their tether. They may be finding it difficult to sell their current property or perhaps they cannot find the right new home. There may be problems with finances, unsettled children or pets or potentially bad neighbours. They tell me about anxiety attacks, sleepless nights and even family arguments. They are often so terrified of making a huge and costly mistake it's surprising they are bothering at all, but of course, there are all sorts of reasons for moving home, not all of them pleasant.

While some people may need a bigger home for their family, or have to relocate because of work, or may be planning to move to a place where they've always wanted to live, I am increasingly seeing people whose property issues arise from divorce, or from being unable to afford their beloved home, or who are selling the home of a parent who has recently passed on. The emotional toll can be huge.

Since property is the biggest investment of most people's lives, you simply you cannot afford to get it wrong. By the time people come to see me they have often tied themselves in knots over finding the right property, location or type of house. Luckily, I can help them find the best possible property, saving them a lot of stress and anguish.

When dealing with property matters, I rarely need to look at the past; it is usually simply a case of finding the ideal place, by taking people forward to see their ideal property. But occasionally I meet a client who has made a series of terrible blunders and then I need to find out if this could be the result of a pattern from the past. Constance was one of these unfortunate people.

Constance's Story

Every few years Constance would move house and each time she would be upset, worried and stressed. I asked her why she didn't save herself the trouble and simply find one good place and settle down. She said, 'It just never happens that way. Every time I find a place I like, within a short while I am itching to move again.'

My instincts told me the problem lay in her past, so I took her back to find the source of her itch to move.

Constance went back to a distant past life when she belonged to a nomadic tribe. Staying in one place was impossible; they could only survive by constantly moving to find new pastures.

In our discussion afterwards, Constance agreed that she no longer needed to keep moving in order to survive, but that she did love the excitement of seeing new places. So rather than continually moving, she decided to make sure she had an adventurous holiday each year.

GLIMPSE YOUR DREAM HOME

For most people, simply catching a glimpse of their ideal home and its location can save them wasting time looking at properties that fall through or turn out to be unsuitable.

Karl and Gilly's Story

Karl and Gilly have been clients of mine for many years. I've watched them grow from humble beginnings and build up their business through hard work and a little insight.

They popped in to see me because they were about to sign a contract for some new business premises and Gilly was having one of her little niggles – she had a strong feeling that something was wrong, but had no idea what. Karl, on the other hand, was adamant that it would be foolish not to snap up what looked like a good opportunity. Usually they agreed on such matters, but whenever they didn't they would see me for the casting vote.

Karl and Gilly ran children's nurseries and had built a great reputation in that field. They'd worked hard and, apart from basic living expenses, had ploughed all the profits back into the business. They were now looking to open a third nursery, which would take every penny they had saved and tie them into a long lease. But they had found the perfect building in the best possible location. So what could possibly be wrong?

Gilly said, 'Maybe it's too perfect, I don't know – but something is holding me back.'

Karl said, 'I just can't imagine finding anything better.'

My own instincts told me there was a major problem with this property and I decided to take them forward together as a couple. They were very in tune with each other and we thought we might get more information this way.

I took them forward two years for them to see what would happen if they took the property.

Karl was the first to speak. He sounded shocked. 'We are not in the building at all!'

'Did you ever set up in the building?'

'Yes, we set it all up and spent a fortune, but it has been closed down. This is terrible. There is a structural problem. The foundations weren't built properly. The builders knew this; they lied to get it past the authorities. Now we are paying the price.'

At this point Gilly chipped in, 'Apparently other people had checked out the building before and found the problem, which is why it has been empty for so long and at such a low price. That should have been a clue for us.'

'What could you have done differently?'

Karl said, 'Ha, well not taken on the place at all! But we should also have asked around first. We didn't think of that, but I bet the locals know something.'

Gilly said, 'This is a disaster, we will lose everything if we go ahead. We would end up bankrupt.'

'Okay, come back to your present time and now take another pathway, one where you make a better decision for your business.'

Gilly looked much happier as she said, 'We have some fantastic new premises and the place is working really well. It has everything we need.'

'Where is it?'

'I'm not sure of the location. It's in a little high street, but it could be anywhere.'

'Karl, can you get an idea on this?'

'I think so. I don't know the place either, but I get a feeling it's about five miles north of our first nursery. I'll have to look it up on a map.'

After the session Gilly and Karl sat quietly stunned. Karl said, 'I really don't know what to make of all that. It seems so far-fetched, yet what I saw was so real. All we can do is check it all out.'

Karl called a few weeks later. He told me, 'I went to speak to a local farmer who confirmed that other people had had surveys done on the place and found a problem. He advised me to steer clear – the owners are known in the area and no local person would ever rent or lease from them.' Karl said they had now found their new premises, close to where Karl had seen, and were 'over the moon'. Gilly, who was also on the call, said, 'And when we were with you, I saw myself carrying our second child at the time we move in, so we also know exactly when to expect our next addition to the family!'

EXERCISE: YOUR IDEAL HOME MEDITATION

Find yourself a place to relax, turn off your phone and make sure you will not be disturbed. Open yourself up, following the instruction on p. xxix.

Take a moment to focus on your breathing and to think about where you are living right now and the reasons why you want to move.

Now just imagine you have settled down to sleep in your current home. You are not going to actually fall asleep, but just imagine that you are sleeping. In fact, this will be a very special relaxation. You will simply drift, and as you do so you will be aware that something is different about this relaxation; somehow, you are tapping into something special.

There is a part of you that can access your own future. So just drift and allow this part of you to open up. You may like to imagine it opening just like a rosebud until it blossoms into a beautiful rose. As you focus on the rose opening you know that this aspect of you is also opening, ready for you to view the future.

As you relax, you get a sense that you are moving forward in time. At this stage you do not know how far forward you are moving – you are simply aware that you are moving forward in time.

You are moving forward towards a time when you will be living in your new home.

Take a moment to focus on time moving forward.

Now be aware that the time has passed and you are now living in your new home. In your mind's eye be aware of waking up in your new bedroom. Get a sense of what it is like; what colours are there? What furnishings?

How does your new home feel? Is it a new property or old? Does it feel cosy, bright, funky? Just allow the thoughts to come to you.

Take some time to get a good sense of your new home.

Now expand your awareness – you can move around and go and see the rest of the house.

How about the outside? Do you have a garden?

Get a sense of the wider scene: where is your home? Is the environment rural or urban? Is it what you want? Are the people nearby friendly?

Now get a sense of how much time has passed. One year? Two years? Or maybe a few months?

Are you happy with what you sense?

Now it is time to leave your future home, so float back to your present time and your present home with a greater sense of where you will be living in the future.

Remember to close yourself down at the end of the exercise (see pp. xxix–xxx).

(If you would like a free download of this meditation, visit www.futurelifeproperties.com.)

Paul's Story

Paul had been house-hunting for some time when at last he found a house that fitted the desired profile. He told me, 'It was a really nice little house in an area I liked, and the price was right. But somehow I had this niggle that wouldn't go away; my intuition was telling me something wasn't right, so I decided to have an FLP session to try to find out if there was anything I needed to be aware of. I wasn't really sure what to expect, but thought it was worth a try.'

Paul has written his own account of what happened next:

'Anne took me forward to a point where I had been living in the house a year, and she asked me if the house was okay.

'I remember saying, "Yes the house is fine."

'Then she asked, "Are you happy?" and I surprised myself by saying, "No". There was no logical reason. I couldn't say the neighbours were terrible or the house had bad vibes; I just didn't feel right there.

'Anne then took me forward again, but this time, as she did so, she told me to find myself in my ideal home. Straight away I could feel I was somewhere different. Then the images came: it was a lovely little cottage and definitely in a different area. This time I had a really happy feeling and knew it was the right place for me. Then I got a sense of roughly where the cottage was.

'Anne then took me forward five years and I saw the property I'll be living in. It's not the property I'm currently in; it's in the same area, but even bigger and it's just as lovely as the place I'm in now!

'I was due to sign contracts on the first property the very next day, but the session had made me realise this was not the home for me. Armed with this information I went in search of my new home and amazingly I found it. I now live in the very home I saw and I love it. I even know where I will be living next!'

––––––––––––––––

When I asked my Future Self what we need to know about abundance, instead of replying directly she told me this parable:

One day the scientists on Earth received a message from a far-off planet. The message was, 'Our life is very harsh. There are just 200 of us and we are struggling to survive. Our instincts draw us to your planet. Please can we come to live with you? We will work hard and share whatever knowledge we can.'

The scientists replied, 'It is very harsh here too. Our weather is constantly changing. We have too many people already. There are wars and pollution. We too are struggling but you are welcome to come.'

It took several months for the people to arrive from their planet and when they did they were dumbfounded by what they found. They told the scientists and governments, 'But you said life was a struggle, and that you have very little, and the people fight and the weather is tough, and that you have too many people.'

They showed them a picture of their own planet which was cold, bleak and barren. They described how their people died young, and were now so undernourished they were no longer able to have offspring.

They said, 'Do you not realise that your planet is

magical! In so many places you have food that pops out of the ground, you have the sun to warm you, and you have the most precious commodity of all – water that falls from the sky.

'And you have children to make you laugh and bring you love; you have elders full of wisdom.

'You have so much, yet so little, because you do not know how to appreciate and share what you have. For us this is heaven and the most abundant planet in the universe.'

A MESSAGE ON ABUNDANCE FROM MY FUTURE SELF

Many people believe that only by becoming wealthy will they be truly happy. In reality, many people who become rich find their lives hollow and empty. Wealth can bring many benefits, but true happiness comes from living life in the right way, by making a difference and by creating something very special. Then you really will be rich.

The final chapter will give you the missing piece of the jigsaw – how to create a wonderful world for yourself and others, and for future generations: your own legacy for the world.

CHAPTER 7

CREATING THE
BEST POSSIBLE WORLD

Throughout this book we have been working on clearing our pasts to bring about a better future for ourselves. Many of us today are worried about not only our own future, but that of the whole planet. As each and every one of us clears our past, the collective energy of the planet becomes a little clearer, which, in turn, helps to create a better future for all. But is there more that we can do?

Can we influence what happens to our world? Is our planet heading for disaster? Will it end up polluted and war-torn or can it become a clean and peaceful haven? Some people think it is already too late in the face of ever-growing populations and dwindling resources, not to mention civil unrest, as well as economic and environmental crises. Are they right?

What is the best possible future for the world and how do we achieve it? There are many pathways our world can take. Now, more than ever, some of us are aware that we hold the key and can influence our collective future. By connecting with our future selves and observing the best possible future of the planet we can gain the answers that will enable us to create a stronger and more positive world.

CAN WE CHANGE THE CONSCIOUSNESS OF THE PLANET?

If enough people focus on the best possible future of the world we can begin to create it. It only needs a small percentage of the population to change their thinking for the change to spread to the rest.

The Tipping Point

In 1960 Maharishi Mahesh Yogi predicted that 1 per cent of a population practising transcendental meditation (TM) would produce measurable improvements in the quality of life for the whole population. Research published in over 100 scientific journals confirms the 'Maharishi Effect'. For example, a study of a random sample of 160 US cities (published in the *Journal of Mind and Behavior* in 1989) found that increasing the numbers of TM participants in these cities over a seven-year period was followed by reductions in crime rates. The study used data from the FBI Uniform Crime Index total and controlled for other variables known to affect crime. More recently, in 2011, scientists at Rensselaer Polytechnic Institute, New York (a private research university) found that when just 10 per cent of a population holds an unshakeable belief, their belief will always be adopted by the majority of the society. According to

▶

Professor Boleslaw Szymanski at Rensselaer, 'When the number of committed opinion holders is below 10 per cent, there is no visible progress in the spread of ideas … Once that number grows above 10 per cent, the idea spreads like flame.' As an example, the events of the Arab Spring in Tunisia and Egypt that began in December 2010 appeared to exhibit this process, with dictators who had been in power for decades suddenly overthrown in a few weeks.

THE STUDY: VISIONS OF THE FUTURE FROM ACROSS THE WORLD

In *The Future is Yours* I described a study I conducted into how the world will be in 100 years' time. Soon after the book was published, my Future Self informed me that it was now time to take a deeper look at the future of our planet, not only to see how it will be, but also to find a better and more positive path towards the future. We wanted to find out what we need to know in order to bring about the best possible future for the planet and for ourselves. What will we be doing differently in the more positive future?

As well as taking my own journeys into our best possible future, I have been working with both groups and individuals to find the answers. My Future Self had told me that the right people would appear, and that key individuals would be guided to contact me by their own far distant Future Selves. It turned out that many of those whose visions I describe in this chapter contacted me spontaneously, telling me they were drawn to my work; often they had dreamt about me or come across my book 'by chance'. Some of them would mention something I was working on privately, or had had visions similar to mine.

My Future Self told me this was simply the starting point and that many more people would join us. Our visions of the future would show us the way, and then it would be up to us to make it happen. She said, 'You draw the people together to create the change the world so badly needs.'

I began to receive invitations to take my work abroad. It was as if, one by one, key places were opening up, all very different from each other, starting with Kuwait, Estonia, Japan and Norway. Each time the pattern was the same: I would be contacted by someone from abroad who would say, 'You must come to my country. We need your work to find our way forward.' It seemed as though certain countries were suddenly waking up to the idea that there is a different way to be and that we have the power to create wonderful change. Each person who contacted me would introduce my work to a larger audience.

During each of my visits I wanted to hear people's visions of the world in fifty years' time and how we can create the best possible future. So I took everyone who came to my seminars or training courses through the Alternative World exercise you will find on pp. 230–3. As well as the group exercises, I also sometimes worked with individuals, when I felt strongly drawn to do so. My Future Self had emphasised the crucial importance of our present time, and I was curious to see if others had the same world visions as me.

As I worked with each person or group I asked them to

keep their impressions secret. We needed to have a clear view and not be influenced by what others had discovered. Time and again the findings were incredibly similar, and I will shortly be sharing some of them with you. But first I needed to look for myself.

MY OWN VISION

My Future Self took me by the hand and we flew upwards until we were looking down on the Earth. She said, 'This is your world in fifty years' time if the people carry on with their current mindsets.'

As I looked down on our future planet I could feel that it was permeated with tension: people were still rushing around frantically as they went about their business. There was pollution in some parts of the world, but other areas seemed cleaner, much cleaner. I scanned the Earth and saw that the air was cleanest around northern Europe, where it was almost sweet. Parts of the Far East such as Japan had clean air, but others were very polluted. I sensed that the clean areas of the world had embraced some new form of energy, and there was also some technology that appeared to actually clean the air.

I was then drawn to Africa, which was far less populated than it is now; I realised that many people had moved to West Africa. At first I wondered if a major catastrophe may have caused such a massive migration, but it seemed there had been a great incentive to move – people were being offered a better life there. I could see there was war in one part of Africa towards the east, and unrest in another, while parts of the continent seemed almost empty.

The Middle East felt peaceful and there seemed to be fewer people, with some areas abandoned altogether. By now there was very little oil, but other resources had been found. There was one small conflict over territory, but no major war. The previous wealth from oil had been put to good use and key areas had been made into centres for business, medicine, science and leisure.

Australia and New Zealand were both prosperous. They had made key decisions and their policies had paid off. America had a pollution problem, but the economy was levelling out after another crash in or around 2029. People were beginning to opt for a simpler life. Again there were fewer people.

The world's weather was still a little crazy – stormier and colder, with no sign of global warming; in fact, the reverse seemed to be happening. And although rainfall had increased, it needed a lot of treatment before it was drinkable, so there appeared to be a global water shortage. There was panic concerning some countries where the drinking water carried bacteria, and I could see a lot of blame being directed at the governments who had caused sickness by refusing to take advice about cleaning their water.

Looking down on the people at this time, I could sense they were tired. There were no dramatic reasons for this, but they needed positive change. They all wanted the same thing: they wanted life to be easier, but somehow they all seemed to be stuck in the same rut.

I asked my Future Self what they needed to do to change things. She replied, 'Let's look at the best possible future for the world. Let's find out how it is different and what the people need to do right now in order for it to happen.'

My view of the best possible future for the world
in fifty years

We spun out into space; then, suddenly, I felt a shudder reverberate through the universe. We swept back down and again looked at the Earth.

This time things feel very different, and I immediately have a sense of harmony peace and good health. In this best possible future, politically things look much better. Strong alliances have been formed and now, instead of individual countries or continents there are groups of countries in alliances, similar to the set-up of the European Union today. Each alliance works closely with the others; the emphasis is on working together and being mutually beneficial. As a result, the world economy is now far more stable.

Again I could see that northern Europe has clean air, but now this extends to more countries. They have developed a number of ways to clean the air and ensure they have fresh water to drink. The Nordic countries have pulled away from the European group and formed their own alliance; they are prosperous and peaceful.

There is still concern over water, but a number of systems have been put into place both to ensure that the air and environment are clean and the rainwater good enough to use after minimal treatment, and to clean any polluted water. The major concern now is to help those countries that heedlessly refused early help.

The systems of government have changed dramatically. Whereas today's politicians stand to reap great rewards, especially financial, under the future system they earn modest salaries. Their expenses are paid, but they no longer use big hotels and claim huge expenses paid for by the people. In the best possible future the politicians use basic hotels and travel economy class.

This has produced a massive change and attracted a completely different kind of politician, people who genuinely want to make a difference. Those who nowadays would be drawn to politics go instead into industry or business to feed their egos and ambitions.

As I wonder how such a system would come about, my Future Self shows me how the people have taken more control. They have stood up and complained more. They have started electing leaders with spiritual values, not easily influenced by big business and men in grey suits.

The Arab Spring has been followed by further uprisings in several countries. People's attitudes began to transform as they realised that collectively they could create change and that politicians were only in power by the grace of the people. They were no longer prepared to sit back and be controlled.

England fifty years ahead feels calmer. People are less stressed and more self-reliant; many have opted for a simpler way of life. They live comfortably, but modestly, and need and want a lot less. The population is smaller because a lot of people have resettled abroad, wanting to build their own self-sufficient lifestyle.

The various alliances have finally embraced new energy systems, and with no disputes over resources, wars have come to an end. Clean energy is no longer hidden away and is now freely available to all.

I have become aware of one particular person, a Gandhi-like figure. I see that he is a very tall, highly evolved man; I wonder if he is the future Dalai Lama, but am not sure. He is softly spoken, but with an air of authority that makes his listeners sit up and take notice. He has told the people: 'Once you know that your neighbour wants the same thing as you, the result is unity. We cannot achieve it by being separate.'

He has shown people how to work together to create a better world for each individual as well as for everyone as a whole. He has taught them to have a war-time spirit in peacetime, so that we work together to make the world a wonderful place for all.

I am overjoyed to find I could communicate with him, and he gives me this message: 'Lead a simpler life. No one needs fifty pairs of shoes or three cars. If everyone just has what they need, there will be plenty.

'Do not put in power people who impress because they are good at rhetoric. Put in power people who will really make a difference: those who ask for nothing for themselves. Be aware of those who are simply furthering their ambitions.'

My Future Self adds, 'You will be visiting several different countries and certain people will be drawn to you. Take time to find out what the people see for themselves. That will set things in motion.'

I started with my contacts in the UK.

VIEWS FROM ENGLAND IN FIFTY YEARS' TIME

My first port of call was Dave, the soldier I mentioned earlier in the book (see p. 43). We have worked together many times and together caught many glimpses of world events to come. Now it was time for Dave to look for a better future.

Dave's view of the world in fifty years, if we stay on our present course

There is no conflict, and the world economy is run differently. The atmosphere is much cleaner, mainly because there is less waste, and the weather is cooler. There are many different types of fuel, controlled by local governments. Population control has reduced the population.

Dave's view of the best possible future for the world in fifty years

There is more individual freedom and less interference from governments. The pace of living is slower – currently there is too much change.

Systems of government are very different from today, with groups of countries working successfully together. Armies are kept to a minimum for non-threatening pur- poses such as helping with disasters. The change has been brought about by the people, who have reached a limit as to what they will put up with and have taken back control to create their own democratic governments and have more say and responsibility in public affairs. Politicians are more accountable.

The change has already started and will be rapid; it is being brought about by the young people growing up now who have a different energy, a new awareness. There is also one man, probably from the Far East, who teaches us to be uni- versal, to be self-sufficient and to embrace the new – to find a better way for the world.

There is one main world economy, but with different economies within it. We are using money in a different way, and free energy is set to revolutionise the world in many ways. The people are more family orientated; they benefit from using technology wisely, and have more time.

> You will have far more control as soon as the people take responsibility for what happens. It is up to us, everyone having their own part to play. It is time for the human race to grow up.
>
> **A MESSAGE FOR THE PEOPLE FROM**
> **DAVE'S FUTURE SELF**

VIEWS OF THE MIDDLE EAST IN FIFTY YEARS' TIME

The first person to contact me from abroad was Eman in Kuwait; she had read my book, *The Future is Yours*, and told me it had changed her life. In 2007 she invited me to visit Kuwait; many people there wanted to ensure that their country, and indeed the whole Middle East, would find a peaceful solution to their current problems, she said. I appeared on their biggest morning TV show several times and in numerous magazines. My books took the top slots for weeks, and I have returned there every year since then.

Below is a compilation of the visions of my Kuwaiti seminar participants.

The Middle East in fifty years, if we stay on our present course

Overall, the Middle East is far more peaceful than it is today, but there is still some slight tension between Egypt, Morocco and Lebanon. Yemen seems to be a cause for concern.

According to my delegates the wrong people are in power

in Egypt and Morocco, and while unity with other countries has been offered, they are concerned with keeping control. Advice offered by other countries about health and clean water has been ignored and now the people are becoming sick. People are struggling financially, since both countries have become more isolated, causing a reduction in trade.

Luckily, around this time a shift occurs: many of my delegates mentioned a huge scandal exposing some of those in power, resulting in new and better governments and rulers.

The best possible future for the Middle East in fifty years

My delegates reported a wonderful feeling of calm and peace in the Middle East: differences have been dissolved and the countries are working in harmony.

The Middle East has become more environmentally aware, now opting to use natural resources. Saudi Arabia has found a way to store solar energy, which is being passed on to the colder countries. The environment looks clean. Many trees are being planted and beautiful landscapes created, coupled with stunningly designed, tall, modern buildings.

A group of Kuwaiti business people is encouraging businesses abroad to cooperate with each other. Qatar has changed its name and is now extremely wealthy; it wields a lot of influence in the Middle East which it uses to break down borders to make travel and business easier. Their motto is 'The land is God's land' and they are promoting the acceptance of all beliefs and faiths. There is a symbol of two people's hands clasped together in unity; this symbol was mentioned over and over again.

A VIEW FROM ESTONIA IN FIFTY YEARS' TIME

My next contact abroad was an Estonian woman named Kreet. She flew into London to meet me and told me, 'I must study FLP with you!' So in 2011 I visited Estonia, a small country with a big vision, and worked for two whole days with a huge group of people. Both Kreet and I were invited on a prime-time television show and were featured in many magazines.

I sent Kreet a recording of the Alternative World exercise (see pp. 230–3), asking her to focus on Europe and her own country, and she emailed me her findings.

Kreet's view of Estonia in fifty years, if we stay on our present course

There is a lot of pollution and much of the land cannot be used for growing food. There is a lack of pure drinking water. The European Union no longer functions. Estonia is doing better than most because we have thought ahead.

Kreet's view of the best possible future for Europe in fifty years

There is far more life in the Nordic countries with greater freedom and fewer boundaries. People have become more spiritually evolved and are more relaxed and aware. We have discovered alternative sources of energy and are using organic agriculture. The environment is well cared for and clean, but not sterile. The energy of the Earth is more balanced. In Estonia, we are combining alternative and conventional medicine.

VIEWS OF JAPAN IN FIFTY YEARS' TIME

Soon after meeting Kreet, I was contacted by a Japanese woman, Sayaka, who told me, 'Your book must be published in Japan and you must come here. The Japanese people need to know their way forward.' Within six months my book was on the shelves in Japan, where it became the top-selling spiritual book. When I visited Japan Sayaka and I were interviewed by numerous magazines and I trained a group of people to become FLP practitioners. I visited Japan again in 2012 and met with further groups wanting to find a way to make their country a peaceful, affluent haven.

I found the people were very keen to know the future of their own country and, indeed, the world. They had suffered a lot and there was a high rate of depression. There had been a lot of fear since the earthquake in March 2011 that resulted in a huge tsunami and the deaths of over 15,000 people. I wanted to help them find some answers.

Below are the findings of the study I did with my Japanese students.

Japan in fifty years, if we stay on our present course

The overall view is of a Japanese people who look miserable with a higher rate of depression. The weather is gloomy and the air polluted. Parts of the country have become desert-like and many people have moved to the countryside, which is no longer green, but brown. Ice is melting from the mountain tops.

People are lonely and feel isolated. They rush home from work instead of socialising. They have little faith in politicians, who admit they do not know what to do. About a third of the delegates see a cloud of polluting yellow dust floating towards Japan. Many mention a natural disaster that drives people to live in the north and west of the country. However, they also see Japan looking into natural energy and making some breakthroughs, giving the nation some real hope.

The best possible future for Japan in fifty years

There is a new breed of politicians who believe in living in harmony with nature. One particular man, the mayor of a major city, is leading the way and changing people's thinking. He encourages industries to put back into society and supports younger people in helping to shape the future. Several people mention Mr Hashimoto, the present mayor of Osaka, as the person who will lead the new direction.

A great many people referred to Japan having free energy which has created clean air; many independently see a large building with the words 'THE FREE ENERGY COMPANY' on it. Japan has explored and funded huge, world-changing discoveries with free energy. Many other countries have sought its help, which has made the country very wealthy. The energy has two sources. Firstly, a grid has been placed out in space which sends energy to the Earth. The second source is through harnessing the power of volcanoes.

Life is easier; people socialise more and make sure the elderly are included and made to feel useful. People have become very aware of nature and many new trees have been planted.

*

I was astonished to hear so many accounts of different subjects and areas regarding Japan in the future, but overall, more than half the delegates came up with the same images. I asked what had brought about such a change in Japan. They told me, 'The opinion of the people brought a change when things reached a tipping point. The people worked together to create a healthier, happier, safer Japan.'

I felt that I wanted more in-depth information about the future of Japan, so I asked two key people who I felt could provide this: Sayaka, who is an organiser of spiritual seminars in Tokyo, and Tomoya Nakamura, a young businessman. Tomoya is an innovative young man with his finger on the pulse; he became successful in business at an early age, but is also spiritually very aware. I told him nothing about the previous day's findings in the group and both he and Sayaka agreed to go through the process of looking at alternative futures with me.

Sayaka's view of Japan in fifty years, if we stay on our present course

I am drawn to Tokyo. People are less passive, and are standing up for what they believe is right. They are not happy about the distribution of wealth. I can see fewer people in the city; many have moved out to the countryside to create a more self-sufficient and harmonious life. This has a direct effect on the prosperity of Tokyo. The economy in general has also slowed down.

The environment is chaotic and unsettled. There is pollution, but not like the usual from factories: it is like a grey-yellow dust coming from another country – it feels like something has gone wrong. And this dust is odd – it affects people's minds and gives them a distorted reality.

Sayaka's view of the best possible future for Japan in fifty years

As I focus on Japan I feel happy and excited. It seems brighter; the sky and sea are a beautiful blue. There is a wonderful balance and integration of the traditional and the modern. I can see very exciting things about the environment. Mount Fuji, the volcano, is being used to create energy. There is also another safe source of energy, like an energetic mesh surrounding the Earth. Somehow it controls the air pressure and weather patterns.

Now, instead of having a centralised government, there is a group made up of different parties which works for the higher good of everyone. They are not your usual politicians; they are young, creative and positive. The new system has been mainly brought about by young men and women. There are two young people who have great influence. One is an entertainer – in music, I think. He has great charisma; the other is a sportsperson. And there is a young guy, casually dressed; he is not political, but because of him the consciousness is being changed. The main message for Japan is that these young people will change the way we think to create a better future for all. All we need to do is to listen to them and help them.

Tomoya's view of Japan in fifty years, if we stay on our present course

My first impression of Japan is that it lacks vitality, it is emotionless. The people are flat. The government has a rigid system. The economy is somehow flat also. Pollution seems to be under control and I see no conflict with other countries.

The main challenge is that the people need to find their joy, something within them. They are fearful.

Tomoya's view of the best possible future for Japan in fifty years

People are so much happier. I hear the laughter! The government has created a new system that encourages more fun, helping people to discover themselves and not worry so much. There is a very young prime minister with a great sense of humour. He is not from a powerful or political family, but he has lived abroad and has learnt a lot by mixing with different cultures and making friends all over the world. He knows there is a way to make this country wonderful. In the previous vision of the future the government was not in touch with the people, but this man knows how to connect politicians to their true selves, and they have a nationwide project to create a good country.

Osaka will be the driving force. One particular person there will make a difference, the mayor, Mr Hashimoto; he wants to create a new system. But the real change comes from young people taking a stand. They make sure the right people are now in power. And we have a green energy which has been created right here.

The Japanese people must keep communicating with each other. Talk to the people around them about deeper things. We need to remember that we have the power to create the future.

A VIEW OF NORWAY IN FIFTY YEARS' TIME

Late in 2012 there was a sudden big wave of interest in my work from Norway. I received numerous emails from

Norwegian people wanting to train as FLP practitioners; indeed, many flew into London to train with me. The view below was given by Marianne, one of my regular clients, who focused on her own country. She downloaded the Alternative World exercise (see pp. 230–3), and sent me her findings.

Marianne's view of Norway in fifty years, if we stay on our present course

My first impressions are of stormy weather along the coastline. It is grey and rainy, a non-descript season, as if the seasons don't exist in the same way as before. My focus then shifts to the woods, which look unhealthy with skinny, weathered trees. I don't see any birds or animals. People aren't spending much time in nature; they look bored, and there is a lack of human warmth. Some highly advanced vehicles have been designed that go very deep into the oceans; at these depths the sea looks very polluted.

Marianne's view of the best possible future for Norway in fifty years

I see a lot of snow and everywhere feels very peaceful. Now the woods feel clean, almost like before the age of industrialisation. And the seasons are back! There is a deep feeling of calm. People are less rushed; there is a growing understanding that the most important thing is to 'own' your own time.

A special group of pioneers has contributed to this alternative future, partly through legislation to stop pollution. They are a new and stronger revival of the Slow Living Movement. Some of the change has come about through protests and lobbying. Progress in science is not made public, but I see improved and revolutionary heating and energy systems which result in Mother Nature suffering far less.

THE STUDY: CONCLUSIONS

It was heart-warming to see how many people had visions that were similar to my own and to each other's. It was encouraging that so many people came up with alternative sources of energy and ways of dealing with pollution, as well as more cooperation between people and governments, and between different countries.

The findings of the study clearly show us our choice of futures: we can do nothing, and the world will limp along into a polluted and unhappy future, or we can create a wonderful future for ourselves and for nature, by changing our values and working together. Over and over, the message was loud and clear: focus on what is truly important. A clean and healthy environment is more important than lots of possessions. And most importantly, make time for what truly matters in life – ourselves and our families – instead of looking for constant entertainment.

In the past people believed that world events were out of their hands; today, increasingly, people are coming to the conclusion that they have a voice and that what they think and do will make a difference. Young people in particular will lead nations to a new way of running governments.

I asked my Future Self for a message for my readers. She told me: 'No one needs to do anything drastic. Just simple changes in the way you think and live. A small shift in priorities is all that is needed. Grow healthy food, support those who make a difference, do not have what you do not need. That is all it takes.

'*Value each other and know that some people are not as far down the road as you are, so be patient. Just give them a little nudge in the right direction from time to time.*

'*You want a good life, of course. You want love, health and success, but many people have the mistaken belief that these are at odds with making the world a better place. In fact, unless you set your purpose and goals for the benefit of the planet and the people, you will be out of alignment and your path will be a struggle.*

'*As you walk your path, you will be joined by others and soon the world will reach the tipping point where a new and better age will begin. All you need to do is play your own part and all will be well.*'

A MESSAGE FROM MY FUTURE SELF

OUR ALTERNATIVE FUTURE WORLD

The fact that you are reading this book may mean that you are one of the key players and pioneers in the destiny of the world. The exercise below will enable you to take a look at our possible futures. In fact, there has been so much interest in this that I have put the exercise on our website as a free download, at: http://www.futurelifeprogression.co.uk/future-of-the-world

EXERCISE: OUR ALTERNATIVE WORLD

Start by opening yourself up, following the instructions on p. xxix.

You find yourself standing outside a hi-tech cinema complex that rises high into the sky like a huge skyscraper. The complex is built in a misty, dark, reflective glass and is adorned with vast screens showing excerpts from the films you can see inside. The screens show footage of our world from outer space, with shooting stars flying across the night sky and grand landscapes.

Across the entrance to the complex is written in huge letters:

THE MOST ADVANCED CINEMA IN THE UNIVERSE
ANY TIME & ANY PLACE

People are hurrying in and out of the cinema, or looking up at the posters, deciding what they want to see. The foyer is bustling with activity as happy customers buy tickets or popcorn and drinks. You realise that this cinema not only shows the usual kind of movies; it also shows you real events from the future.

An usherette approaches you and hands you a golden ticket. She tells you that with this ticket you can go anywhere you wish.

She waves her hand towards the lifts. You step inside one, reach forward and press the button and suddenly, with a whoosh, you feel yourself being carried rapidly upwards.

Then the movement slows down and the lift comes to a gentle stop. The doors open straight into a large cinema. An usherette directs you past many rows of seats to a big, soft, cosy chair at the front. You settle down and make yourself comfortable, just as the screen comes to life.

Projected across the screen are the words:

OUR WORLD IN FIFTY YEARS' TIME

Underneath, a subtitle reads:

IF WE STAY ON OUR PRESENT COURSE

And now you are looking down on the world from outer space in fifty years' time.

Notice where your attention is drawn to. Do any countries stand out? Are you drawn to landscapes, cities or maybe the sea?

Suddenly, the scene flows out from the screen and surrounds you; you can even walk around and pull places to you. You are standing inside a holographic image and you can go anywhere in the blink of an eye. You only need to think it and you will be there.

Just with the power of your own mind you can float back out and look down on the world, or you can zoom in and go anywhere you wish. This truly is the most amazing cinema in the universe.

Float out and look down on the world. How are things in fifty years' time? Are you drawn to a certain place? Just let it happen and allow the information to flow to you.

How is the world economy?

Which countries are thriving and which are struggling?

How is the environment?

Is there any pollution?

What is the weather like?

Are there any wars or conflicts? Notice where you are drawn to.

How are the people? Have they grown spiritually? Have they evolved?

What are the main issues and challenges facing the world?

Have there been any breakthroughs – in science, medicine or technology, for example?

Is there anything else we need to know?

And now allow the images to settle back into the screen.

Take a nice, deep breath as the images on the screen fade away.

Next, the usherette smiles and tells you that you are about to see something very special.

A new message appears on the screen:

THE BEST POSSIBLE FUTURE FOR THE WORLD IN FIFTY YEARS

An image of the Earth fills the screen. Again, you notice where your attention is drawn to – perhaps a country or city, maybe the countryside or oceans – and a scene projects out around you. You are standing in the middle of a holographic image of the best possible future of our world.

Notice what is different about this future from the last one.

How does it feel?

Have there been any significant events?

How is the world economy? Have there been any break-throughs?

How is the environment?

What is different about the world? What have we done differently?

Who is making a real difference? Is there any one person or group who has helped to make this the best possible world?

Accept what comes to you.

Now ask: what do we need to know that will help us to create the best possible future for our planet?

Again, take whatever comes to you.

Have one long last look at the best possible Earth. Absorb the energy. How does it feel?

How do the people feel? Capture that feeling and keep it with you. Hold it in your hand. You can grab a big chunk of that positive energy in your hand and hold it tight.

Keep holding on to that energy as the holographic images flow back to the screen.

Float back to the present time and, as you arrive back in the present, open your hand and feel that energy spread out and grow: it keeps growing and spreading positive energy all over the world, and somehow you feel a little different and the world feels a little different, and somehow you know things are beginning to shift towards a brighter, better future.

End by closing yourself down, as usual (see pp. xxix–xxx).

When you have gone through the exercise above, we would love to hear your findings, so do paste them on to our Facebook page and connect with our community: http://www. facebook.com/pages/Future-Life-Progression/12373872 4303587. Alternatively, you can email your findings to us (info.annejirsch@gmail.com) and we will add them to the website.

To participate in creating a better future for all, please feel free to do the exercise above (as well as the one overleaf) with friends or in groups. Group meditations can be very powerful. Or you can simply pass them on to friends who may like to join in.

CONNECTING WITH THE VIBRATIONS
OF THE EARTH

The following exercise will help you to take your next step by aligning you with our beautiful planet and its own special vibration. So far, throughout this book, we have slipped around in time as we have cleared the past and created a better future. Now the Earth energy will connect you to the here and now; to this point in time when you find whatever your own special mission is in the great scheme of things.

EXERCISE: CONNECTING WITH THE EARTH

Start, as usual, by opening yourself up (see p. xxix).

Imagine you are standing out in nature on a beautiful day. Stand tall and be aware of the ground beneath your feet. Take time to focus on your surroundings on this beautiful planet. Wherever you are right now, be aware of the vast oceans and seas, the mountains, forests, jungles and deserts, the cities, towns and villages. Be conscious of all the people and creatures that live upon the Earth and know that everything has a part to play, even the tiniest insect.

Know that the Earth is a form of energy and has a consciousness of its own.

Feel the aliveness of the planet and notice how it has its own special vibration; it is subtle, but if you stop for a moment to be still and mindful, you will feel it.

As you connect to the vibration of the Earth, your own vibration will strengthen.

Now allow your energy to flow down into the Earth, blending with the Earth's own vibration.

As your energy flows down to the Earth, feel the Earth's energy flow back up to you.

Now allow your aura to grow bigger and bigger and brighter and brighter until it is flowing around the entire Earth, sending beautiful energy for the good of all.

Just know that as your energy flows outwards it will positively influence others, and as they are influenced they will, in turn, influence even more people. The ripple effect will spread further and further.

Know that each and every positive thought and action that you take will ripple out to others and down to the centre of the Earth, down to the deepest point on Earth and will then flow outwards to every inch of the planet.

Your vibration will also flow to the past and to the future, creating more and more positive vibrations, influencing people everywhere; the four corners of the Earth, the past and future. Flowing to your ancestors and those yet to be born.

It will flow into the universe where it will carry on creating positive energy for infinity.

As you stand upon the Earth, know that your smallest contribution will make a difference. It will do more than you can ever imagine.

You were born with a special awareness that is needed at this crucial time in history. You know you came here to learn and grow, but also be aware of your contribution. Allow the answers to flow up from the Earth.

Be aware of why you are here and your mission on Earth, and know that you are far more powerful than you can ever imagine. As you return to your everyday life keep this awareness with you to guide you each and every day.

Remember to close yourself down, following the instructions on pp. xxix–xxx.

THE SNOWFLAKE

One day My Future Self and I flew to the top of a mountain. As we landed, snow began to fall. She told me to hold out my hand and a snowflake landed in the centre of my outstretched palm. She said:

'That snowflake is just like each and every person on Earth. You are all unique, but as single entities you are very fragile.' At that moment the snowflake melted in my hand. 'You see, a lone snowflake is gone in the blink of an eye.'

She then held out her hand and caught one flake after another. Soon her hand was piled high with snow.

She said: 'As more and more snowflakes join together, they become more and more powerful, until finally they can create an avalanche.

'A snowflake is like a moment in time: unless that time is spent wisely it will run through your fingers and be gone for ever. Each moment is too precious to waste. Join with others to become the avalanche, and make every moment count now for the past and for the future.'

CONTACTING THE AUTHOR

To contact Anne Jirsch, please email: info.annejirsch@gmail.com. Or you can visit her website at: www.annejirsch.com

For more information on Future Life Progression, to access free downloads or find your nearest practitioner go to: www.futurelifeprogression.com

BIBLIOGRAPHY

Diaz, Luis Angel, *Memory in the Cells*, Universe Inc., 2010

Jirsch, Anne, *The Future is Yours*, Piatkus Books, 2007

Jowett, Benjamin, *Collected Works of Plato*, Oxford University Press, 1953

Loftus, E. F. and Doyle, J. M., *Eyewitness Testimony: Civil and Criminal*, 3rd edition, Harvard University Press, 1997

McKenna, Paul, *I Can Make You Rich*, Bantam Press, 2007

Schacter, Prof. Daniel, L. (ed.), *Memory Distortion: How Minds, Brains, and Societies Reconstruct the Past*, Harvard University Press, 1997

Schacter, Prof. Daniel, L., *The Seven Sins of Memory: How the Mind Forgets and Remembers*, Houghton Mifflin, 2001

Shaputis, Kathleen, *The Crowded Nest Syndrome: Surviving the Return of Adult Children*, Clutter Fairy Publishing, 2004

Sheldrake, Rupert, *A New Science of Life*, Park Street Press, 1981; revised new edition, Icon Books Ltd, 2009

Sheldrake, Rupert, *The Presence of the Past*, Icon Books Ltd, 2011

Skynner, Robin and Cleese, John, *Families and How to Survive Them*, Methuen, 1983

Treffert, Darold, A., MD, *Extraordinary People: Understanding Savant Syndrome*, Bantam Press, 1989; updated edition, Backinprint.com, 2006

Van Gennep, Arnold, *Les Rites de Passage*, 1909; first English version: *The Rites of Passage*, Routledge & Kegan Paul, 1960

Wambach, Helen, *Life Before Life*, Bantam Press, 1984

Wambach, Helen, *Reliving Past Lives: The Evidence Under Hypnosis*, Bantam Books, 1979; HarperCollins 1985

Wolf, Fred Alan, *The Yoga of Time Travel*, Quest Books, 2004

RESOURCES

Foreword

Dr Paul McKenna: www.paulmckenna.com

Introduction

FLP Facebook page: http://www.facebook.com/pages/Future-Life-Progression/123738724303587 FLP website: www.futurelife progression.com

Free download – London in Ten Years' Time: http://www.futurelife progression.co.uk/london_in_10_years.php

Chapter 1

The Barefoot Doctor: www.barefootdoctorglobal.com

Dr Rupert Sheldrake: www.sheldrake.org

Dr Dean Radin: www.deanradin.com

Chapter 2

For FLP practitioners: www.pflsociety.org

Chapter 3

For Eating Problems

BEAT (Beating Eating Disorders) www.b-eat.co.uk

MIND, the Mental Health Charity: infoline 0300 123 3393, www.mind.org.uk

Anorexia and Bulimia Care (ABC): www.anorexiabulimiacare.org.uk

For Internet Addiction

Dr Kimberly Young, Clinical Director, Center for Internet Addiction Recovery: www.netaddiction.com

The Priory Group: tel. 0845 867 3953; http://www.priorygroup.com/addiction-anxiety-depression-treatment

Gamblers Anonymous: www.gamblersanonymous.org.uk

For Drug Addictions and Alcoholism

MIND, the Mental Health Charity: infoline 0300123 3393; http://www.mind.org.uk/mental_health_a-z/7992_addiction_and_dependency

Alcoholics Anonymous: www.alcoholics-anonymous.org.uk/

Narcotics Anonymous: www.ukna.org/

Free healing download: www.annejirsch.com/spiritual-healing-energy.php

Chapter 4

Free past-life download: http://www.annejirsch.com/cds-and-downloads.php

Chapter 6

Laurelle Shanti Gaia: www.reikiclasses.com

Free download of Your 'Future Home': www.futurelifeproperties.com

Chapter 7

Maharishi University of Management, 1000 N 4th St, Fairfield, IA 52557, USA; tel. (641) 472 7000; www.mum.edu

Pippa Jackson, Energy Alliance Practitioner, Advanced FLP Practitioner: www.the-amber-room.com

Kreet Rosin: www.kreetrosin.com

Free download of The 'Best Possible Future for the World': http://www.annejirsch.com/future-of-the-world-download

The Study: please send your feedback to the FLP Facebook page: http://www.facebook.com/pages/Future-Life-Progression/123738724303587

INDEX

Also by Anne Jirsch:

COSMIC ENERGY

How to harness the invisible power around you
to transform your life

Foreword by Paul McKenna

In *Cosmic Energy*, top psychic Anne Jirsch teaches
you how to harness the pure power of the universe to
attract health, wealth and happiness into your life.

Her special tools and techniques will help you tap into
your own energy and the energy around you to:

- Reveal your life's purpose
- Attract positive people into your life
- Secure the perfect job and improve your business
- Connect to all the wealth and happiness in the world
- Maximise your wellbeing – and that of your loved one

In her friendly, accessible style, Anne teaches you how to
tap into the cosmos to transform your life.

978-0-7499-5325-6

INSTANT INTUITION

A psychic's guide to finding answers
to life's important questions

Anne Jirsch

In *Instant Intuition*, Anne Jirsch reveals her own unique
techniques for effortlessly developing clairvoyant ability.
As you follow Anne's fascinating life story, she describes –
with practical and straightforward exercises – how
you too can switch on your psychic skills.

Instant Intuition will give you the tools to find quick
access to life's compelling questions about love,
relationships, work and success. It also explains:

- Anne's revolutionary Etheric Energy Techniques
  (E.E.T). These methods will enable you to tap into
  a person's thoughts and emotions – no matter where
  they are in the world.
- How you can travel into your own future using
  Anne's tried-and-tested techniques of Future Life
  Progression (FLP). If you don't like what fate has in
  store for you, you can act now to change your
  destiny.

Instant Intuition is packed with real life stories, simple and
effective psychic exercises, quizzes and case studies and
will help you to transform your life – with instant results!

978-0-7499-2921-3